Thespian Playworks 2014

The Trial of Adbot 579
by Francis Bass

What We Talk About When We Talk About Planned Parenthood
by Alexa Derman

This Play is About Pirates
by Caleigh Derreberry

Skin
by Derick Edgren

A Samuel French Acting Edition

SAMUELFRENCH.COM
SAMUELFRENCH-LONDON.CO.UK

THE TRIAL OF ADBOT 579 Copyright © 2014, 2015 by Francis Bass
WHAT WE TALK ABOUT WHEN WE TALK ABOUT PLANNED PARENTHOOD Copyright © 2014, 2015 by Alexa Derman
THIS PLAY IS ABOUT PIRATES Copyright © 2014, 2015 by Caleigh Derreberry
SKIN Copyright © 2014, 2015 by Derick Edgren

All Rights Reserved.

Cover Images © by Susan Doremus

THESPIAN PLAYWORKS 2014 is fully protected under the copyright laws of the United States of America, the British Commonwealth, including Canada, and all other countries of the Copyright Union. All rights, including professional and amateur stage productions, recitation, lecturing, public reading, motion picture, radio broadcasting, television and the rights of translation into foreign languages are strictly reserved.

ISBN 978-0-573-70456-7

www.SamuelFrench.com
www.SamuelFrench-London.co.uk

For Production Enquiries

United States and Canada
Info@SamuelFrench.com
1-866-598-8449

United Kingdom and Europe
Plays@SamuelFrench-London.co.uk
020-7255-4302

Each title is subject to availability from Samuel French, depending upon country of performance. Please be aware that *THESPIAN PLAYWORKS 2014* may not be licensed by Samuel French in your territory. Professional and amateur producers should contact the nearest Samuel French office or licensing partner to verify availability.

CAUTION: Professional and amateur producers are hereby warned that *THESPIAN PLAYWORKS 2014* is subject to a licensing fee. Publication of this play(s) does not imply availability for performance. Both amateurs and professionals considering a production are strongly advised to apply to Samuel French before starting rehearsals, advertising, or booking a theatre. A licensing fee must be paid whether the title(s) is presented for charity or gain and whether or not admission is charged. Professional/Stock licensing fees are quoted upon application to Samuel French.

No one shall make any changes in this title(s) for the purpose of production. No part of this book may be reproduced, stored in a retrieval system, or transmitted in any form, by any means, now known or yet to be invented, including mechanical, electronic, photocopying, recording, videotaping, or otherwise, without the prior written permission of the publisher. No one shall upload this title(s), or part of this title(s), to any social media websites.

For all enquiries regarding motion picture, television, and other media rights, please contact Samuel French.

MUSIC USE NOTE

Licensees are solely responsible for obtaining formal written permission from copyright owners to use copyrighted music in the performance of this play and are strongly cautioned to do so. If no such permission is obtained by the licensee, then the licensee must use only original music that the licensee owns and controls. Licensees are solely responsible and liable for all music clearances and shall indemnify the copyright owners of the play(s) and their licensing agent, Samuel French, against any costs, expenses, losses and liabilities arising from the use of music by licensees. Please contact the appropriate music licensing authority in your territory for the rights to any incidental music.

IMPORTANT BILLING AND CREDIT REQUIREMENTS

If you have obtained performance rights to this title, please refer to your licensing agreement for important billing and credit requirements.

FOREWORD

It's a lonely gig, being a teenage playwright in a typical American high school. You can try to fit in with the rest of the *homo sapiens adulescens*, do your best to mimic their appearance and behavior, but as soon as you start talking, writing, *thinking*, it's obvious: you're a whole other species.

Maybe that's one reason all four Thespian Playworks 2014 winners feature characters who might be called, for various reasons, *the other*. Pirates of the Midwest, robots for hire, a seal-girl who's lost her pelt, a pair of drug-addicted lovers who've done the unspeakable – these are the kinds of outcast beings a young playwright can understand.

Of course, the plights of characters living on the margins are also inherently dramatic. Will the pirate make good – or turn bad? Will the commercial-spouting robot reveal a soul within? Will the selkie save her own hide, or sacrifice it to another? Can the young, strung-out couple finally forgive themselves and grow up? These are the stories that came to life in June, over a week of workshop rehearsals and staged readings at the Thespian Festival in Lincoln, Nebraska.

It was a rare opportunity for the authors – Caleigh Derreberry from Brookwood High School in Lilburn, Georgia, who wrote *This Play Is About Pirates*; Francis Bass, from Leon High School in Tallahassee, Florida, author of *The Trial of Adbot 579*; Derick Edgren from Auburn High School, Rockford, Illinois, who wrote *Skin*; and Alexa Derman from Westfield High School in Westfield, New Jersey, author of *What We Talk About When We Talk About Planned Parenthood* – to break out of isolation and to work with people who clearly loved their plays as much as they did.

"Everything about the week was amazing," Derreberry said. "It was such a great experience, but I think the best part was just being with Alexa and Francis and Derick, hanging out with them, going to workshops together or talking about what had gone on in rehearsal that day. My light-bulb moment was realizing that there are other people out there who appreciate plays and want to write them. Where I come from, I don't know anyone else who wants to do that."

"My school doesn't have any kind of writing classes or clubs, really," echoed Bass, who, like Derreberry, wrote his play pretty much in secret, after many false starts. "I don't know any other writers.... Going to this and seeing what it's actually like to see your play up on its feet – I definitely want to get into that more."

The students, now attending various colleges, *have* gotten into that more, I'm glad to report: Derman recently wrote to tell me about a New York production of her latest script, and the others have shared similar successes. Their Playworks plays live on as well, thanks to our friends at Samuel French, Inc., a major supporter of the program since 2009. We at *Dramatics* and the Educational Theatre Association are especially grateful for this handsome acting edition, part of a growing Playworks collection. Here is physical proof that when it comes to a passion for original, theatrical storytelling, these young writers are not alone.

– Julie York Coppens

Senior Associate Editor, Dramatics Magazine

CONTENTS

The Trial of Adbot 579 9
What We Talk About When We Talk About Planned Parenthood 35
This Play is About Pirates. 53
Skin 83

The Trial of Adbot 579

by

Francis Bass

THE TRIAL OF ADBOT 579 was presented in a staged reading as part of the Thespian Playworks program at the 2014 Thespian Festival on June 28, 2014. Bill Myatt directed, Judy GeBauer served as dramaturg, and Lydia Shirley served as stage manager. The cast was as follows:

ADBOT 579	Tom Sawyer
VICTORIA ANDERS	Katherine Blauvelt
DANIEL PIKEMAN	Micah Zelmetz
JUDGE DUNBAR	Katherine Pereira
DR. RUSSELL	Evan O'Rourke
ADBOT X-58	Andrew Bates

ABOUT THE PLAYWRIGHT

Francis Bass wrote *The Trial of Adbot 579* in his junior year at Leon High School, in Tallahassee, Florida. Soon he'll be enrolled at the University of Iowa, where he'll pursue an English major through the creative writing track. The stage-ability and overall polish of the version of his play published here is owed to the excellent guidance of Bill Myatt and Judy GeBauer. Francis thanks his family for never asking him to pursue a practical career, Roderick Durham for his feedback and encouragement from freshman year to now, and most of all Eden Rush for being an outstanding influence and inspirer. This play is dedicated to her.

CHARACTERS

ADBOT 579 – Earnest, generous, and easy to strike up a conversation with. He seems driven by a desire to help others.

VICTORIA ANDERS – Almost maternally protective of Adbot 579, she can let this protectiveness overcome her in heated moments.

DANIEL PIKEMAN – Wise-cracking, rather callous, and in love with the sound of his own voice.

JUDGE DUNBAR – Formal. Tries to keep the proceedings professional.

DOCTOR RUSSELL – Very awkward, has difficulty socializing. He is driven by curiosity and a desire to report his findings.

ADBOT X-58 – Condescending, uncaring, and excessively posh.

SETTING

City Hall, a meeting room.

AUTHOR'S NOTE

The frame of this play takes place in a meeting room in city hall, during a hearing. However, the core of the play occurs in a bar, as Anders (the bar owner) and Pikeman (legal representative for Annons Co., the fictional manufacturer of Adbot 579) testify and narrate the action. When the other characters freeze, Anders and Pikeman become the Anders and Pikeman of the present, testifying to the court. When they unfreeze, the two become the Anders and Pikeman of the past, in the bar. The distinction between these two settings – the bar and the courtroom, past and present – can be accomplished with a lighting change or sound cue, or something else I'm not clever enough to think of.

(Two tables at either end of the stage are slightly slanted to run upstage toward the center. These two tables have about five feet of space between each other at center, and are slightly downstage. Each table is made of two square tables, to make long rectangles. There are two chairs behind the stage left table. At edge of stage, center, is a chair facing upstage.)

(At rise: **VICTORIA ANDERS** *sits behind left table in right chair with papers spread before her. She is well dressed but not overly formal.* **ADBOT 579** *sits at right of* **ANDERS**, *with similar attire.)*

ANDERS. Don't worry, 579, we've got this.

579. Oh – pff, come on. You know I don't worry.

ANDERS. Well don't, because there's no way we lose this one.

579. Who're you telling, Tory – me, or yourself?

ANDERS. What are you, my therapist?

579. You got a therapist?

ANDERS. No, I was joking, I don't have a therapist. *(Pause.)* See – right there, we got this.

579. What are you talking about?

ANDERS. A normal adbot would've pounced on that, would've advertised some therapist company or something. But you didn't.

579. Therapist company? The hell is a therapist company?

ANDERS. It's a…it's like a…

(**DANIEL PIKEMAN** *enters left with a briefcase. He wears a gray suit. He stops by* **579**.)

PIKEMAN. You gotta be kidding me.

ANDERS. Hello again.

PIKEMAN. *(Pointing at* **579**.*)* He can't be here.

ANDERS. What? Why not? This whole thing is about him!

PIKEMAN. It's illegal. *(Goes to the other table.)*

ANDERS. Illegal to – to have him here?

579. Why?

PIKEMAN. *(As he opens his briefcase and organizes some papers.)* Yes, the law states that the adbot on trial cannot be present. Seeing the actual adbot might sway the judge's sympathy. *(To 579:)* Now leave – go outside and tell the pedestrians about…great deals on vacuum cleaners or whatever.

(**579** *exits left.* **JUDGE DUNBAR** *enters right, and, seeing her,* **ANDERS** *stands. She is dressed formally.* **JUDGE** *stands before the chair at edge of stage, holding a notebook.*)

Are we ready to begin?

JUDGE. *(She might speak into a microphone.)* Yes. I, Judge Dunbar, call this trial to order, to decide whether or not Adbot Five Hundred Seventy-Nine is "indistinguishably human," and therefore cannot be scrapped for parts. The prosecution will make their argument, then the defense –

PIKEMAN. All right, can we stop acting like this is a real trial. The "prosecution"? This is the place where they have AA meetings, not the Supreme Court.

JUDGE. Then the defense will have a rebuttal. The defense will make their argument, then the prosecution will rebut, and each side will have closing arguments. Understand?

ANDERS. Sure.

(**JUDGE** *goes to her chair at center and sits down.*)

PIKEMAN. All right, I'll start off by saying that it is impossible for an adbot to be self-aware, one of the defining qualities of –

ANDERS. What are you talking about?

JUDGE. Ms. Anders, you will have your turn.

ANDERS. Objection, lying.

PIKEMAN. Objection, this is not a real court.

(**ANDERS** *looks plaintively to* **JUDGE**.)

JUDGE. "Lying" isn't even something you can object about. Prosecution, continue.

PIKEMAN. As I was saying, it is impossible for an adbot to be –

ANDERS. And as I was saying, that is a blatant lie. Ma'am, it is entirely possible for an adbot to become self-aware, by running a routine to check contradictions in their promotional files. The more promotional files, the more often these checks are run.

JUDGE. You're quite informed for a bartender.

ANDERS. Uh, thank you.

PIKEMAN. But there's more to a human than checking promotional file whatevers. So I'll start off with the fact that Adbot 579's speech is completely robotic.

ANDERS. What? His speech is just fine, it's –

JUDGE. Ms. Anders, you will have your opportunity to –

ANDERS. His speech sounds less robotic than Judge Dunbar's – no offense.

JUDGE. That –

PIKEMAN. I don't mean the tone, I mean what he says. I have a few examples here, if you'd like.

ANDERS. Wait – you can't just quote Five out of context.

JUDGE. Ms. Anders –

PIKEMAN. Really, "context"? Fine – *(To* **JUDGE.***)* Picture this "context."

(As he speaks, the lights dim to a less harsh, more natural quality. The bar is brought on, stools are placed around it. It sits roughly center stage.)

An old, greasy bar with mismatched glasses at it, spotted with watermark rings. A few creaky stools are pulled up to it, matching the bar's old, worn-out condition. Tables are…

ANDERS. All right, enough – I meant what we were talking about, not what my bar looks like.

JUDGE. Would you two like to completely abandon the trial format and just talk at me until you don't have anything to say, or –

ANDERS. Yeah, sure.

PIKEMAN. Fine.

JUDGE. *(After a pause.)* I suppose that would go faster anyway. Carry on.

ANDERS. Right, so here's the context you actually need.

*(As she continues, **579** enters, goes behind bar, and freezes while cleaning a glass. **PIKEMAN** goes off right.)*

At about midday, Mr. Pikeman and an AI specialist arrived, as scheduled, to perform a series of standard tests.

*(**579** unfreezes and cleans the glass as **ANDERS** takes a seat at one of the tables. **PIKEMAN** and **DOCTOR RUSSELL** enter at right. **RUSSELL** wears khakis and a dress shirt that has been poorly tucked in. He holds a spiral-bound notebook and pencil. Throughout the play, **RUSSELL** will often write in the notebook.)*

PIKEMAN. *(As they walk to the bar.)* Hello, I'm Daniel Pikeman, the legal representative from Annons Co. This is our AI expert, Doctor Russell.

*(**579** puts out his hand to shake. **PIKEMAN** passes him, going to **ANDERS**.)*

RUSSELL. *(Stops at right of bar, apart from the others.)* Hi.

ANDERS. *(Stands and shakes **PIKEMAN**'s hand.)* Hello, I'm Victoria Anders, renter of Adbot 579.

PIKEMAN. So you want to keep your old adbot because you think it's human.

ANDERS. He is human.

PIKEMAN. You do know that it's impossible for an adbot to be self-aware, right?

RUSSELL. Actually, they can run a routine to check contradictions in their promotional files. The more promotional files, the more often these checks are run. It's a type of self-awareness.

PIKEMAN. *(Sarcastic.)* Thanks for that. Even so, they don't have any personality.

ANDERS. You would've been right eight years ago, when I first got 579. But thousands of promo installations later, he does have a personality. I mean, you must have seen this before, right.

PIKEMAN. As a matter of fact we have never seen anyone hold onto an adbot for eight years. How cheap are you?

ANDERS. *(Quickly walking past* **PIKEMAN***, to* **RUSSELL***.)* But if someone did, this makes sense right?

RUSSELL. Well, the promotional files program in an affinity for the product they're promoting. So if you have enough of them installed, you'd start to see trends, and these trends could be analogous to trends in personality.

PIKEMAN. Fun facts aside, your adbot is worth more to us as spare parts. Advertisers don't want to have one of these older models peddling their wares, they want the newer One-K bots – so here's our offer. We'd like to replace your old adbot with a new one, free of charge.

579. *(Finished cleaning glasses.)* Um, duh, it's free of charge. We pay for ourselves with advertisements, that's the point.

ANDERS. Well, there's still an initial fee.

579. Really? How much was I?

ANDERS. No offense…about a thousand.

579. Wow…that's almost as cheap as the new augmented reality glasses from Electronics Conglomerated – boy, those things just get cheaper and cheaper, huh?

*(***579** *and* **RUSSELL** *freeze.* **PIKEMAN** *turns to audience to address the* **JUDGE***.)*

PIKEMAN. And that, Judge Dunbar, is example number one. Example number two, and I quote, "Pyramid Pale Ale is real hoppy but not so bitter it makes you choke. It's got a good balance you don't find in most IPAs, a great choice for any beer drinker looking for more than the typical domestic brews."

ANDERS. *(To* **JUDGE***.)* Now hold on – he's taking this out of context again. When Five said it – well, the doctor guy was running through this script for a normal conversation –

RUSSELL. *(He and* **579** *unfreeze. To* **579.***)* All right, just act like I'm any old customer.

(Walks to bar and sits down. He pulls a script out of the notebook and sets the notebook on the bar. **ANDERS** *sits nearby.)*

579. So, what can I get you?

RUSSELL. *(Simultaneously, reading from script.)* Did you see the game last night.

*(***RUSSELL** *stares at* **579** *like a deer in headlights.)*

579. Which game?

(Long pause as **RUSSELL** *stares intently at script.)*

RUSSELL. The Broncos.

579. Oh, against the Patriots. Yeah, I did. That was just ugly, huh? What a mess.

RUSSELL. Yeah, great touchdowns. *(Pause.)* What would you recommend?

579. To drink?

RUSSELL. To drink.

579. Well that depends. We've got a wide selection of beers –

RUSSELL. Yes. A beer.

579. Well, Pyramid Pale Ale is real hoppy but not so bitter it makes you choke. It's got a good balance you don't find in most IPAs, a great choice for any beer drinker looking for more than the typical domestic brews.

*(***579** *and* **RUSSELL** *freeze.)*

ANDERS. See, a normal thing to say to a customer.

PIKEMAN. Well the list doesn't end there. The doctor's "normal conversation" wasn't working out, so I stepped in.

*(***579** *and* **RUSSELL** *unfreeze.* **PIKEMAN** *sits at the left side of the bar.)*

What's a guy got to do to get a drink around here?

579. *(To* **RUSSELL.***)* You figure out what you want, I'm gonna talk to this guy.

RUSSELL. *(Flipping frantically through notebook, looking for an answer to this eventuality.)* Uh…

579. *(To* **PIKEMAN.***)* What would you like to drink?

PIKEMAN. Scotch, neat, expensive.

579. *(Fixing the drink.)* Here you are.

PIKEMAN. Thanks, and keep these coming.

579. Rough day?

PIKEMAN. I've had to deal with this imbecile at work who's got to tag along with me.

RUSSELL. I'll have that beer you suggested.

*(***579*** digs around beneath the counter, then finds the bottle and puts it down before* **RUSSELL.** *He turns back to* **PIKEMAN** *as* **RUSSELL** *scans through his papers.)*

RUSSELL. Thank you. *(He continues riffling through the script.)*

PIKEMAN. It's like this guy has never been in the real world before.

579. I hear that. I used to work with this adbot who was just a moron. Didn't even say "hi" to a person before he was spewing out names of car dealerships.

PIKEMAN. Uh-huh.

579. So, are you from around here?

PIKEMAN. No.

RUSSELL. *(Almost simultaneously.)* No.

579. *(Ignoring* **RUSSELL.***)* If you haven't found a place yet, the Hampton Inn off Meridian Street is a quite affordable and well-furnished hotel to stay in.

*(***579*** and* **RUSSELL** *freeze.)*

PIKEMAN. Which would be example number three.

(They unfreeze.)

Great, excellent.

RUSSELL. *(Having finally found a place in his notebook.)* So, this is some strange weather, isn't it?

579. *(Turning to* **RUSSELL.***)* I guess. If rain is strange.

PIKEMAN. *(Leaning over bar, to* **RUSSELL.***)* It's not. I don't know what you're talking about. It rains here all the time.

579. *(Turning back to* **PIKEMAN.***)* I thought you said you were from out of town.

PIKEMAN. *(After struggling to think of something.)* Shut up.

579. Hey man, what's the matter?

(Seeing **PIKEMAN** *get more and more flustered.)*

You finish that off, we'll talk it out. *(Turning to* **RUSSELL.***)* What's this about the weather?

RUSSELL. The…the snowstorm.

ANDERS. Snowstorm? It's midsummer. How old is that notebook?

PIKEMAN. That doesn't matter.

RUSSELL. Four and a half years.

ANDERS. You should update it.

579. Are we still doing –

PIKEMAN. Yes, we are. *(To* **ANDERS.***)* And don't interrupt. *(To* **579.***)* You seen my car?

579. The yellow convertible? It's hard not to see it. What kind of insurance do you have on that guy?

PIKEMAN. I think that'll do here.

*(***579** *and* **RUSSELL** *freeze.* **PIKEMAN** *stands. Walking downstage:)*

When has a real bartender ever asked you about your insurance? This is not how a human talks, this is not how a human behaves. His end goal in any conversation is to advertise a product.

ANDERS. *(Stands. Moving to bar to stand by* **579.***)* That is not true. Well, he's an adbot, he can't help advertising, but he does it for the sake of the people, not the product. He really does care about them, to the point where he actually remembers most people he talks to.

(She heads left.)

I brought in an adbot that used to work with us to show that.

(**579** *and* **RUSSELL** *unfreeze.* **ANDERS** *walks Adbot* **X-58** *on from left.*)

This is Adbot X-58.

(**ANDERS** *and* **X-58** *stop by upstage left table.* **X-58** *is dressed in a polo shirt and khakis.* **579** *comes out from behind the bar.* **PIKEMAN** *and* **RUSSELL** *move to stand by upstage right table,* **RUSSELL** *taking his notebook from the bar.*)

PIKEMAN. X-58? That's one of our premium models. You didn't keep him?

ANDERS. The customers were so used to Five that they found X-58 to be a bit too –

X-58. (*Passing* **579** *and going up to* **PIKEMAN**.) Your suit appears a tad bit empty at the elbows. Alonso's Suits and Ties can craft for you a tailor-made suit at a doesn't-quite-fit price. Alonso's Suits and Ties. Look more than just your best.

(*He walks past a slightly peeved* **PIKEMAN** *to* **RUSSELL**.)

A few squirts of Caballero Body Spray go a long way. Caballero Body Spray – the long-lasting deodorant for a gentleman.

RUSSELL. Thank you. (*Writes in notebook.*)

X-58. (*Turns and takes a few steps away from* **RUSSELL** *and* **PIKEMAN**. *To* **ANDERS**.) What am I to do here?

ANDERS. You and Five can just…catch up.

579. Do we have to?

(**ANDERS** *looks at him as if to say, "You know you have to."* **579** *continues, with forced amicability.*)

Um, hi, X-58.

X-58. You're Adbot Five Hundred Seventy-Nine.

579. Yeah, Five-Seven-Nine.

X-58. Ah yes, this is where I worked before I moved on to the Garden Creek Country Club. I see you still tend bar at this hole in the wall.

579. (*Walking up to* **X-58**.) I do. Look, I know we weren't best friends when we worked here, but –

X-58. I do not care.

579. Exactly what I'm saying. Even though we –

X-58. I mean I know nothing of that, because I have ceased to care about anything that happened here.

579. Oh. Well, I'm glad to see you, to get a chance to catch up, even if people are watching us like some reality TV show.

X-58. You mean like *Dudes on a Boat*, airing this spring on CBS?

579. *(Nostalgic.)* Man, just like old times.

X-58. What is?

579. Are you kidding me? That, what we did just there – I'd set the ad up, you'd take it home – come on, that was our classic play, it was the greatest part of having another adbot.

X-58. I just saw an opportunity to advertise and took it. If you want to be sentimental that is your own business. I am only doing my best to advertise to the middle-classers.

579. *(Sarcastic.)* That must be so tough for you. Advertising to us plebeians. I'm sure you're not used to such a low-class viewership.

X-58. I'm not. *(Strolling past **579** as he advertises.)* You see, the country club is classy, elite. A place for proper men and women to kick back and enjoy what they've earned. Garden Creek Country Club – because high society deserves the best accommodations.

579. Sorry – they have you advertising the country club at the country club?

X-58. Members bring their friends. The friends can be advertised to. Do you mean to tell me that you do not possess a promotional file for this bar, to use for non-regulars?

579. I do, but I don't use it.

X-58. I cannot even respond to that. What kind of an adbot are you?

579. Maybe I'm one with a little class.

X-58. Class, you say? Like the Garden Creek Country Club, a place where –

579. Seriously? How bad is your memory that you can't even –

X-58. My memory is fine. I just do not concern myself with anything that happens in this bar, or outside the country club. Speaking of which, how much longer must I stay here?

ANDERS. You can go now.

(X-58 exits right.)

579. That guy is such a –

(579 and RUSSELL freeze, 579 in mid-speech.)

ANDERS. *(Walking to 579.)* Adbot 579 is remarkably more human than any other adbot you could find. He cares about other people. He remembers them, he builds relationships with them, just like a human. I'd say that makes him indistinguishably human.

PIKEMAN. Now hold on – there're plenty more examples of him being inhuman that I'd love to show you here –

ANDERS. What, like that humor test?

PIKEMAN. Exactly like that. Adbot 579 is humorless. I'll give some examples.

(579 assumes a neutral stance, facing RUSSELL, and then the two unfreeze.)

RUSSELL. Why did the chicken –

(RUSSELL and 579 freeze.)

ANDERS. *(To PIKEMAN.)* Whoa, you're skipping a big chunk there.

PIKEMAN. I just don't want to waste the judge's time here, so I'm giving the abridged version.

ANDERS. The abridged version – you mean the one that makes you look good.

PIKEMAN. I always look good.

ANDERS. So let's tell the long version then.

PIKEMAN. Once again, I don't want to waste time here.

ANDERS. *(Advancing on* **PIKEMAN.***)* Waste time? Five's life is at stake here –

PIKEMAN. *(Meeting her between* **579** *and* **RUSSELL.***)* All right, you can cool it with the histrionics, his life is not at stake because robots don't have lives and nothing is actually at stake. No trial has ever found a single robot to be "indistinguishably human," as the law goes – a law written, by the way, by sci-fi fans who just wanted to live out their childhood fantasies. All it means is any time we want to scrap an adbot and some bleeding heart tries to stop us, we have to go through this whole song and dance about what it means to be human, so why don't you just play along, and we can get out of here sooner.

ANDERS. *(After a pause to calm herself down.)* So here's what really happened.

*(***ANDERS** *and* **PIKEMAN** *part sharply from each other and go to stand where they were before.* **579** *resumes his previous position after his line "That guy is such a – ." He and* **RUSSELL** *unfreeze.)*

579. – jackass. Guy starts working for a rich demographic, thinks he's a distinguished gentlemen.

(As he rants on, **RUSSELL** *takes copious notes.)*

Mr. "Alonso's Suits and Ties," Mr. "Caballero Body Spray" – and calling the stuff cheap. McDonald's is cheap – Walmart is cheap! Alonso's Suit and Ties is…

(As he sees that **RUSSELL** *has been writing:)*

What are you writing?

RUSSELL. *(Absolutely fascinated, thrilled in his own way.)* It's as I suspected. Your programmed affinities for certain products have the emergent property of developing something recognizable as a personality.

(He and **579** *freeze.)*

PIKEMAN. Oh, come on Ms. Anders, get on with it!

ANDERS. I'm just being thorough – *(As an aside to* **JUDGE:***)* But do note that bit about personality.

PIKEMAN. So anyway –

(**RUSSELL** *and* **579** *unfreeze.*)

If you're done scribbling away there, Russell, let's do the humor test.

ANDERS. Humor test?

PIKEMAN. To see if he laughs at jokes.

ANDERS. Of course he can laugh!

579. Yeah, I can –

PIKEMAN. I know he can, but you can laugh at something and not find it funny. This will be a controlled test, eliminating any pity laughter. *(To* **579.***)* Now, Dr. Russell is going to tell you some jokes and you are going to respond, but only if you genuinely find them funny.

(He sits at left of upstage right table.)

RUSSELL. You said you would tell jokes.

PIKEMAN. Change of plans.

ANDERS. Oh come on, tell some jokes. We'd all love to –

PIKEMAN. Russell, you are telling the jokes.

RUSSELL. Oh…okay. *(Takes a second to think of a joke. To* **579***)* Why did the chicken cross the road? To get to the other side.

(Pause.)

ANDERS. Well I don't know how you couldn't laugh at that, Five. I'm in stitches over here.

RUSSELL. Uh, so how do you bury a chemist?

579. How?

RUSSELL. Wait, did I… *(Raises notebook as a nervous tic before realizing it cannot help him.)* Well it still works. Uh, you barium.

ANDERS. That was so –

579. *(Very dry.)* That's the best delivery I've seen since FedEx Priority Shipping.

(**579** *and* **RUSSELL** *freeze.*)

PIKEMAN. Example number five.

ANDERS. Example number one – he told a joke, which speaks more to his humor than him not laughing at terribly delivered, grade-school jokes.

PIKEMAN. *(Ignoring **ANDERS**, standing.)* Adbot 579 did not laugh at a single one of those jokes. He is humorless.

ANDERS. And let's not ignore the fact that you set him up to fail.

PIKEMAN. What?

ANDERS. *(Walking to **PIKEMAN**.)* You obviously made your partner tell the jokes because of how awkward he'd been at the conversation.

PIKEMAN. I made him tell the jokes because – I don't have to justify this to you, let's move on to the next test.

ANDERS. The sacrifice test, really? You're going to call him inhuman for that?

PIKEMAN. Absolutely.

ANDERS. I'll love to see how you spin this.

*(**RUSSELL** and **579** unfreeze.)*

PIKEMAN. All the alarm lines have been turned off?

ANDERS. Yes.

PIKEMAN. *(Walks up to **579**.)* All right then. 579, we're going to go out. Once we leave, we need you to ignore the memory of everything that's gone on here today. You can do that, right?

579. Sure, I can just lock it away, it'll be like it never happened.

ANDERS. Lucky.

PIKEMAN. Then do that, and only unlock the memory when we say the password, "basketball." Got it?

579. Yep.

PIKEMAN. *(To **ANDERS**.)* You go to the backroom throughout all of this, don't come out until we tell you.

ANDERS. Okay.

PIKEMAN. *(As **ANDERS** exits left.)* Let's do this then.

*(He exits right, and **RUSSELL** follows. **579** goes back behind the bar and is about to clean glasses when he*

realizes they are already clean. He is confused for about a second, before the door opens and **RUSSELL** *and* **PIKEMAN** *enter. They are wearing ski masks and holding up handguns, which they point at* **579**.*)*

All right, hands up, barkeep! And come out from behind there.

*(***579** *puts his hands up and walks out from behind bar, standing center stage.* **PIKEMAN** *stands five feet to his right,* **RUSSELL** *downstage a bit and right of* **PIKEMAN**.*)*

Are you the owner of this place?

579. No.

PIKEMAN. Who is?

579. Not me.

PIKEMAN. Is the owner here now?

579. No. She doesn't work Fridays.

PIKEMAN. You're lying. I've been coming here the past four weeks, she's been here every Friday.

579. If you know who the owner of this place is why did you ask me if I was her?

RUSSELL. Yeah, why did –

PIKEMAN. To see if you would lie to someone with a gun. Now we've called your bluff, so really tell us where the owner is, or we'll shoot.

579. No.

PIKEMAN. What, you don't think I'll do it?

579. Sorry.

RUSSELL. *(Lowering gun.)* So do we call it quits?

PIKEMAN. Wha – what?

RUSSELL. I mean, do we just stop now? He's made up his mind, and when an adbot has done that they don't usually change it.

579. You know, I don't recognize that brand of gun, but I can tell you whatever it is it won't compare to the Fletcher's new semi-automatic pistol. Smooth on the recoil with pinpoint accuracy. A Fletcher's shot always hits the mark.

PIKEMAN. You're really going to advertise during a holdup?

579. What kind of gun is that anyway?

PIKEMAN. What does it matter?

579. It matters because I'm almost positive they're fake.

(**PIKEMAN** *glances at* **RUSSELL.**)

PIKEMAN. Well –

(**579** *lunges at* **PIKEMAN**, *tackling him to the ground and throttling him.* **PIKEMAN** *tries to talk but can't, motions to* **RUSSELL** *to say the password.*)

RUSSELL. Uh, uh, uh, what's the password?

(**PIKEMAN**, *after a moment of frustration, mimes shooting a basketball.*)

Uh, uh, arms, outstretched…uh, praying mantis, uh, uh, "Thriller" dance, uh…

(**PIKEMAN** *mimes dribbling.*)

Uh, high five, high fives for everyone, uh, uh…

(*Excited, thinks he really has it.*)

Oh oh oh, patty cake! No?

579. (*To* **RUSSELL.**) You're really not gonna come over here and help this guy? Guess I'll have to do this the hard way.

(*He takes his hands off* **PIKEMAN**'s *neck.* **PIKEMAN** *gasps for air a few times as* **579** *stands and moves to* **RUSSELL.**)

PIKEMAN. Basketball!

(**579** *stops and looks back and forth between* **PIKEMAN** *and* **RUSSELL**, *then stops and starts laughing uproariously.* **579** *and* **RUSSELL** *freeze,* **579** *doubled over laughing.*)

ANDERS. (*Entering left, stopping in front of upstage left table.*) Example number two. He laughed so hard I heard it in the back room.

PIKEMAN. The important point here is that he was willing to sacrifice himself.

ANDERS. Exactly.

PIKEMAN. This makes him inhuman.

ANDERS. What?

PIKEMAN. *(Ignoring* **ANDERS**, *to* **JUDGE**. *Through the course of this line he makes his way to center stage.)* No human would've behaved that way. He probably would've lied initially, but when he got caught he would've given his boss away, because if it comes down between me and my boss – well I'm not the one that got mixed up with criminals, why should I die for my boss's sake? This is how a human would think, but it was not how Adbot 579 thought. *(At center now.)* He is not human.

ANDERS. *(To* **JUDGE**.*)* Self-sacrifice is one of the most human attributes that – look at any other species of animal, they will never cause harm to themselves for the sake of another.

PIKEMAN. *(To* **ANDERS**.*)* Adbots are not a species. We don't slap them on the back for self-sacrifice, we expect it.

ANDERS. Well I guess that means adbots are programmed to be human then, huh?

PIKEMAN. I don't know what kind of fantasy world you're living in –

ANDERS. *(Has already started towards* **PIKEMAN**.*)* Look, just because you're a cold-hearted bastard –

JUDGE. Hey! Calm down! *(Beat.)* Is there any remaining evidence either of you would like to present?

ANDERS. Yes, there is.

*(***579*** assumes a neutral posture, then he and* **RUSSELL** *unfreeze.* **PIKEMAN** *goes to sit at upstage left table, massaging his neck and scowling at* **579**.*)*

RUSSELL. This is our last test. Very simply, we want you to try and empathize with us.

579. Okay. Done.

RUSSELL. What?

579. Well, I'm already empathizing with you. So…do I pass?

RUSSELL. We're going to need more proof than that. So, just go ahead and explain what it is about each of us that you empathize with.

(As 579 talks, RUSSELL will write in his notebook.)

579. *(Turns to ANDERS.)* Well, Tory. I can see you really care about me, almost maternally. Like we're family. And that's why you're trying to prove I'm human, because you want to protect me.

(Turns to RUSSELL.)

Dr. Russell, you, you don't seem really motivated to have me scrapped. You're more interested in learning and being able to tell other people about me, about everything you've learned. You're quite keen on teaching people things.

PIKEMAN. I'll say.

579. *(To PIKEMAN.)* And you, well you know how this whole thing is gonna end, so you're just going through the paces and cracking wise wherever you can. This whole thing is a joke to you, everything we're doing here is just a platform for you to talk. Which you seem to enjoy.

ANDERS. You're dead on. Dr. Russell, would that be an accurate description?

RUSSELL. Certainly.

PIKEMAN. *(This has ruffled him a bit.)* Yeah, sure.

(579 and RUSSELL freeze.)

ANDERS. I defy you to find another adbot with that level of ability at understanding people. You won't. 579 is special, he is caring, compassionate, he has qualities most humans could only aspire to. And he is too human to be killed.

PIKEMAN. *(Standing, emphatically.)* What hypocrisy.

ANDERS. What?

PIKEMAN. I think you're leaving something out, something that hurts your case quite a bit. *(To JUDGE.)* Allow me to elaborate.

(579 and RUSSELL unfreeze.)

ANDERS. See Five, you're different. You're too human, they'll never let you be scrapped.

PIKEMAN. *(Goes to left of* **ANDERS.***)* Hold on. 579, you've been able to describe each of us – our motivations, where we're coming from – why don't you describe yourself.

579. Huh?

PIKEMAN. Just like what you did with each of us.

579. Well, I'm an adbot, so I make recommendations and help people find what they need.

PIKEMAN. That's what you do. Describe why, though, tell us what it's like to be in your shoes.

579. Well, people say I'm –

PIKEMAN. I don't care. What do you say?

*(***579** *stares ahead for a long time.)*

ANDERS. Come on Five, you know this. Do the – run the routine for contradictions, or whatever.

(Silence.)

Five, come on! This is just…

PIKEMAN. *(Smiling.)* You know, this trial hinges on self-awareness. If he can't –

ANDERS. *(Wheeling on* **PIKEMAN.***)* Shut up! You're – stop grinning! Stop it! You're grinning about killing –

PIKEMAN. Killing – like breaking a phone is killing it? How about my juicer, I put too much mango in it and had to throw it out, was I murdering it? Was that death by mango?

ANDERS. Shut up! You asshole, be quiet and just stop smiling!

(Shoves him and he stumbles back a bit. She turns back to **579.** *Beat.)*

Five, please. You've got to.

(Pause.)

579. I can't.

*(***579** *and* **RUSSELL** *freeze.)*

PIKEMAN. I defy you to find a human that can't describe themselves. Which goes back to my original point that he's not really self-aware, not the way a human is. To me, that's a pretty big distinction between 579 and a human.

(Short pause.)

JUDGE. Thank you for presenting your arguments. If you can wait outside the room, I'll come to a decision shortly.

PIKEMAN. All right.

ANDERS. Yes, thank you.

(Lights down. As most of the set is brought offstage, only the portion with 579, PIKEMAN, and ANDERS is lit. ANDERS paces nervously, 579 stands still, and PIKEMAN wears a smug grin and taps his foot. Lights up on an empty stage except for a door at right and a bench near it, facing the audience, behind ANDERS, PIKEMAN, and 579. 579 takes a seat on the bench, and after a short pause JUDGE enters right and walks through the door.)

JUDGE. I've reached a verdict. Adbot 579 has been deemed inhuman.

PIKEMAN. Excellent. *(To ANDERS.)* That is one hell of an adbot, I'll admit. *(About to express some regret at having 579 scrapped.)* You know...

(Decides to say no more, exits left. JUDGE is starting left as well when ANDERS follows after her, dragging 579 with her.)

ANDERS. Judge, Ma'am.

(JUDGE turns around.)

JUDGE. Yes?

ANDERS. Listen, just – just have a conversation with him, please, let him show you –

JUDGE. You made an excellent case. The best I've seen. Your adbot can do things I've never heard of any other doing. But when it comes down to it, your case cannot be the first time an adbot is called indistinguishably human. When that happens, everything will change. And your adbot simply isn't human enough for me to set precedent to save him.

(Looking to **579**.*)*

This is him, isn't it?

579. Hello, Judge…sorry, I don't know your name. They kicked me out before I could find out.

JUDGE. Dunbar.

579. *(Shaking her hand.)* Well, nice to meet you, Judge Dunbar.

JUDGE. *(Cracking a smile.)* It's a good thing I didn't talk to you before the trial. I like you. *(To* **ANDERS**.*)* It's still just an adbot, Ms. Anders.

*(***JUDGE** *exits left, leaving* **ANDERS** *at center stage.)*

579. *(After a pause.)* You know I'm cool with this, right? I'm not being hurt.

ANDERS. *(Heading back to* **579**.*)* You will cease to exist – it's not going to hurt, but you're –

579. Who cares? I'm not afraid of getting disassembled.

ANDERS. *(Stopping at left of bench.)* You really are selfless, huh?

579. I guess.

ANDERS. I mean truly selfless. You actually don't care about yourself at all. That's considered an incredible virtue, and it's…it's why you've been deemed inhuman.

579. Exactly. I don't worry about me, you shouldn't either.

ANDERS. Well you know what? I'm not worried about you, okay. I am human, I am selfish, I don't want you to die, for my own sake, all right? Get it?

579. Yeah.

ANDERS. You know, people say they care about other people. They make friends, they give gifts, they do favors. They just want to feel better about themselves, they like the feeling of helping, of having a friend. It's all for ourselves. That's why you're not human. You help people just to help them. *(Something occurs to her.)* At risk of yourself even.

579. Yep.

ANDERS. *(Quickly sits down next to* **579.***)* You're not going to save yourself for yourself – so save yourself for me.

579. What?

ANDERS. Leave here, go on the run, flee the country, never come back. For me.

(Pause.)

579. If I ran away, it'd be the same – to you – as me dying. Either way you'd never see me again. Only I would benefit, and I don't even –

ANDERS. Humans are stupid. I don't know if it's for me or you or if I'm being selfish or whatever. I just don't want you dead.

(Pause. She is near crying.)

Just tell me. Just tell me you're going to run away. Like you said, you'll be gone either way, I'll never know the difference.

579. Okay then. I'll run away, Tory. I swear, I will.

*(**ANDERS** sits down next to **579** and cries, fighting the tears. **579** puts a hand on her shoulder, comforting. Pause.)*

Man, Kleenex Ultra-Absorbable Tissues sure would come in handy here. Clean you right up, with three tissues or less.

*(**ANDERS** smiles and leans over to hold **579**. Lights fade to black.)*

End of Play

What We Talk About When We Talk About Planned Parenthood

by

Alexa Derman

WHAT WE TALK ABOUT WHEN WE TALK ABOUT PLANNED PARENTHOOD was presented in a staged reading as part of the Thespian Playworks program at the 2014 Thespian Festival on June 28, 2014. Joe Norton was director, Lindsay Price served as dramaturg, and Lydia Pryzybylski served as stage manager. The cast was as follows:

B. .... Gill Vaughn-Spencer
KITTY. .... Allie Sinclair

The play was previously staged as a part of the Blank Theatre's Young Playwrights Festival, also in June of 2014. The production was directed by Andre Barron, with Oahn Ly as a dramaturge and Allison Mamann as stage manager. The cast was as follows:

B. .... Will Rothaar
KITTY. .... Sarah Agor

ABOUT THE PLAYWRIGHT

Alexa Derman is a student at Yale University, majoring in English. Most recently a semifinalist for the Eugene O'Neill National Playwrights Conference, her plays have also been recognized by Young Playwrights Inc's national competition, the Blank Theatre, the National Scholastic Art & Writing Awards, the Playwrights Theatre of New Jersey, and Princeton University. Her solo show *Hamlet & Ophelia* had its NYC premiere with Semicolon Theatre in June 2015. Eternal thanks to family, friends, and the Westfield High School theatre department.

FROM THE EDITORS OF *DRAMATICS MAGAZINE*

This play deals with issues of abortion, drug addiction, codependency, and other mature subjects, and it contains language that might not be suitable for the classroom or school stage. Still, we wanted to share this powerful script with as many of our readers as we could, while honoring the author's expressive rights and intent. In this version, there are five instances in the dialogue where we've asked the playwright to provide alternative language in place of the one word (it begins with an "f") we generally avoid publishing in the magazine; a single instance about halfway through the play remains, because the playwright felt, and we agreed, that any substitute phrase (such as "messed up") would not carry the line's full impact. The rest of the dialogue appears exactly as she wrote it. Readers may request a copy of the unaltered script by emailing editor Julie York Coppens at jycoppens@schooltheatre.org.

CHARACTERS

B – Twenty-something. Dismissive.
KITTY – His girlfriend. Younger, coltish.

AUTHOR'S NOTES

The dialogue should generally move quickly, with characters interrupting each other as indicated. B should avoid raising his voice with Kitty. Until a point, she isn't worth yelling over.

(An apartment. Downstage, a couch. **KITTY** *is underneath it.* **B** *enters, glances around, maybe looks offstage into a bedroom, a bathroom. His pace escalates slightly.)*

B. Kit? Where are you? *(Nothing.)* Kitty? *(Nothing.)* Kitty – where are you? Come on. It isn't funny.

KITTY. I'm over here.

B. What?

KITTY. Over here. Under here.

(He approaches the couch, squats down beside it.)

B. What're you doing under there?

KITTY. Listening to my –

B. You freaked me out. You can't just disa –

KITTY. Pulse.

B. What?

KITTY. My pulse. There's really good acoustics under here.

B. There's about an inch of space above your nose.

KITTY. Cozier that way.

B. You're kidding.

KITTY. It sounds like a thud.

B. Yeah Kitty, it does that – come out from under there.

(Nothing. She's listening.)

Christ.

KITTY. Could you keep it down? I'm trying to –

B. Sorry, should I just leave you to yourself then.

KITTY. That'd be great.

B. How long've you been under there?

KITTY. Years.

(He stands up.)

B. Do I need to call someone?

(**KITTY** *comes out from under the couch. These next few lines occur in rapid succession.*)

KITTY. You messed it up, I –

B. I'm serious. Should I call someone?

KITTY. I wish you would leave me alone.

B. I wish you would start answering my questions and stop being cryptic. Look at me – how much this time?

KITTY. *Zero.*

B. (*Trying to use the calm voice.*) Because we can – I'd understand if you…needed to…after, but –

KITTY. Nuth-ing. None. Leave me alone.

B. You're curled up in the middle of the room, so that's pretty goddamn difficult.

(**KITTY** *looks at him.*)

KITTY. (*Seriously.*) I didn't take anything other than the painkillers. I promise.

B. Fine. (*He relaxes slightly.*) Does it hurt a lot?

KITTY. It hurts okay.

B. And your pulse?

KITTY. I like when it's…deafening. I feel more alive?

B. (*Skeptical.*) Kitty.

KITTY. Plus I'm thinking if mine sounds like *thud* and in the sonogram that sounded like *whoosh* that means it probably wasn't really human anyway so what's the big deal.

(*She goes to move back under the couch, but he stops her.*)

B. You know it only sounded that way because of the machine.

KITTY. But how can we be sure.

B. Is this what you've been doing this whole time?

KITTY. I feel like a scientist. You know. Hypothesizing.

B. Right.

(*He tries to move away. She doesn't let him.*)

KITTY. And like you know if I was going to have an alien baby or something we really dodged a bullet this time, am I right?

B. *(Trying again, curtly.)* Kitty, knock it off.

KITTY. I mean that could've been a disaster. The FBI would probably get involved and we'd never have any privacy again. I mean honestly.

B. *(Shakes her off.)* You're not being funny.

KITTY. I mean we were probably doing good for the human race overall you know because who knows what it could've been – maybe it was like evil or something with that angry alien pulse, like *whoosh, whoosh, whoosh* –

B. Dammit, can't you just stop.

KITTY. I'm not totally sure anymore.

(Silence. KITTY fidgets.)

I mean alternately I'm the inhuman one, and it's supposed to *whoosh*. Let me get yours for comparison.

B. What?

(KITTY moves towards him, puts her ear against his chest and listens. He avoids touching her.)

KITTY. Sort of in between. You're nervous. Why're you nervous?

B. Why do you think?

KITTY. Don't be nervous, baby.

(She goes to kiss him in order to distract him. He stops her.)

B. Can we not?

KITTY. What?

B. Can we not do this thing where you freak out and freak me out and say all kinds of shit and then just…?

KITTY. Just…?

B. And then just go back to us.

KITTY. You don't like us?

(KITTY moves to touch him. B deftly avoids her.)

B. You know it wasn't an alien or something, right, you know it would've been a –

KITTY. Mind your own business.

B. That's what I'm doing. You're my business.

KITTY. Romantic.

B. I mean that.

KITTY. You think I don't know?

B. I think you think whatever you want to think.

KITTY. What do you mean by that.

B. You know what I mean, Kitty.

KITTY. No, enlighten me.

B. *(Tightly.)* You see things how you want to see them.

KITTY. How I want to see them.

B. You turn things into what you want them to be. It's not a big deal, everyone does it, I –

KITTY. You think this is what I want this to be? You think this is what I want to feel?

B. That's not what I'm saying, I just –

KITTY. Because this is something that *happened* to me, it's not something I inflicted upon myself for fun or –

B. That's not what I meant! I thought you wanted to *talk* abou –

KITTY. You know what? I need a cigarette.

(She retrieves one. He laughs.)

(Struggling to light it.) What?

B. Just. You know. Vices. You.

(She takes a drag, offers it to him. He doesn't take it.)

KITTY. Vices. Me.

B. You couldn't smoke if you'd stayed... *(He won't say "pregnant.")* You know that, don't you?

KITTY. Well, it doesn't matter now, does it?

B. And, you did, so...

KITTY. So did you. What about second-hand, and all that?

B. All I'm saying is it's another –

KITTY. Another what?

B. Reason, I guess.

KITTY. What, like a strike – three and you're out? Please tell me more about one and two.

B. You're joking, right?

KITTY. *(Half-sarcastic.)* I'm interested.

B. You're interested.

KITTY. Sure. It's something that happened. I'm interested.

B. You keep saying that – you keep saying, "something that happened," but it's not like that, it's not something that just happened if it's a position you put yourself in and –

KITTY. A position I put myself in.

B. If it's something your actions –

KITTY. Oh, my actions.

B. Yeah, the actions where you can hardly take care of yourself let alone –

KITTY. I take care of myself!

B. Bullshit. You don't eat, you barely sleep, you'll have a cigarette to "take the edge off" and then you put the edge right back on when you –

KITTY. *(Standing up, knowing what's next.)* Let's go out. Wouldn't that be nice? Let's go out.

B. *(Finishing his previous sentence.)* Get high every other night and –

KITTY. No – no, you stop that right now. I'm doing the best I can and I didn't –

B. You said you wanted to know –

KITTY. Listen to me, I'm trying, I swear, I'm trying, you're one to talk, I –

B. I didn't have a kid inside of me.

KITTY. You know I wasn't then, you know that, I made a mistake on Tuesday but with the kid I was clean, don't –

B. Do I really know that?

KITTY. Yes, you do! You know! I told you – right when I found out I told you I was going to do it and –

B. Congratulations, you inhaled a pack a day instead of smoking crack for a whole month.

(She slaps him, then jerks back, surprised. **B** *rubs his face, surprised as well).*

You shouldn't be on your feet.

KITTY. If you think I'm such a raging mess you should go.

B. Kitty.

KITTY. I *knew* that I couldn't do it. That's – why – I – didn't – keep – it. I'm not *stupid*. Did you really think you convinced me to get it done all by yourself? *(Pause.)* You did, didn't you?

B. I don't know what to think.

(She curls up a bit. He touches her shoulder. She jerks away.)

KITTY. I didn't use while – you know. Okay?

B. Okay.

KITTY. Are you going to leave me?

B. Probably not.

KITTY. Okay.

(She moves up against him. He doesn't touch her more than he has to.)

What're you doing?

B. Thinking.

KITTY. About?

B. Things.

KITTY. Descriptive.

B. You. Us. What else.

KITTY. *(Echoing.)* What else.

B. With – what happened, I –

KITTY. You.

B. I just – are you sure I didn't convince you?

KITTY. What?

B. Kitty? Did I convince you?

(She pulls away.)

KITTY. I told you that you didn't.

B. But did you want it?

KITTY. Doesn't matter what I want.

B. You wanted it.

(She stands up, or pulls away further.)

KITTY. Couldn't have handled it.

(The next few lines overlap.)

We're too young. Don't make enough money. I'm –

B. Baby?

KITTY. – a wreck. We aren't married...

B. Kitty, you're using my arguments. Those are my arguments.

KITTY. They're true.

B. *(Seriously.)* I'm sorry.

(She looks away.)

Kit?

KITTY. They're good arguments. I didn't do anything I wasn't comfortable with.

B. You were trying to rationalize ten minutes ago under the couch. You were –

KITTY. I didn't do anything I wasn't comfortable with at the time.

B. What's that mean?

KITTY. Do you ever think how like – like when you're born, there are infinite possibilities for your life, and then every decision you make whittles some away. Moving to some city, dating someone, taking some job – they all shrink those possibilities, cut some out. So like, going to Planned Parenthood was like – I don't know. There were maybe a few thousand different things it could've been and now it's just tissue. Medical waste.

B. I never thought about it like that.

KITTY. I do all the time. And I feel like – like going from thousands to one is disorienting. You know? I feel, like, dizzy almost. It's just frozen there. Now it's always, like, cells. Permanently.

B. But if you think it'd be better that way...

KITTY. And while we're really great and all, it feels strange to think that we have, like, the ability to dwindle something from thousands to one. You know? Like some days I can barely get out of bed without coffee and other days you know I'm shaking – I can't even control what my body does but I can eliminate hundreds and hundreds of possibilities with a couple hundred bucks. Isn't that weird?

B. Maybe a little.

KITTY. I feel like someone mistook me for a tiny God, you know?

B. You're losing me.

KITTY. Like the fact that I'm *so* insignificant but I get to do something so huge – it feels like a cosmic accident.

B. Alright, but this *was* an acc –

KITTY. I wasn't talking about that kind of accident. Don't be crude. You know what I mean.

B. *(Carefully.)* But there weren't hundreds of possibilities. Do you really think if a kid were born into this shitty apartment with our shitty income she'd have infinite different opportunities to be anything other than a wreck?

KITTY. She.

B. Did I just – ?

KITTY. You did.

B. I didn't mean to.

KITTY. Right.

B. Kitty? It was an accident.

KITTY. A girl.

B. I guess I think of you.

KITTY. Hopefully she'd be nothing like me and you don't know it would be a wreck.

B. Educated guess.

KITTY. You can't "educated guess" on a person.

B. With us for its parents? I don't know.

KITTY. What you really mean is with me for a mother.

B. No, that's not what I'm saying.

KITTY. Yes it is. Are you serious? Don't be a jerk. I know that's hard for you but you could at least make an effort.

B. I know it's hard for *you* to remember that we made this decision because you are an addict but you could at least make an effort!

KITTY. I am *not* an addict.

B. Keep telling yourself that.

KITTY. I was clean! I was clean for a month! You watched me – I was shaking and you remember – I was puking and you were holding my hair! I'm not an addict! An addict… I'm not – an addict is –

B. An addict is what? What is an addict, Kitty?

KITTY. *(Immediately.)* Someone who's fucked up past help.

(Beat.)

It was – after. Okay? I was…upset. You know that.

B. Right.

KITTY. Tuesday…it was different.

B. *(Matter-of-fact.)* I know it was different on Tuesday. It was different on Tuesday because you were high when you swore you were through.

KITTY. It was different on Tuesday because I was upset because after we – our *kid* and –

B. You don't think anything else would've upset you for the eighteen years it would've stuck around? You don't think someone in your family would lose a job or get cancer; you don't think we would've fought? You sure you never would've gotten harassed by a stranger or had a falling out with a friend or even a bad day? Stop being ridiculous.

KITTY. If you think I can never ever quit then why don't you just go?

B. If the drugs alone bothered me that much I'd already be gone!

KITTY. Well it's not my fault that you still miss them so badly that you need to do it through me! That's *not* on me.

B. You think I miss that? You think I miss…crawling on the floor looking for more after I've blown through all my cash?

KITTY. I think you miss feeling awesome and happy and whole for ten minutes a day – I think you miss flying. But it's fine – I'm happy to be of service. I hope my cute little mania brightens your goddamn evening and keeps you entertained.

B. That's not true. That's bullshit – I want you to quit, I –

KITTY. Fine. But don't act like me using is such a big deal when it doesn't even matter.

B. You think it doesn't matter? What, are you joking?

KITTY. You just said it didn't bother you!

B. You think this is about me? It doesn't matter if it doesn't bother me – I'm not dependent on you for survival. I can leave you if it ever got so out of control that my safety's in jeopardy. You don't keep me alive or determine my entire development as a human being. Oh, sure, you're pretty hilarious and sexy when you're high, Kitty, even if it makes you a mess – you're entertaining, by all means – but I'm not sitting at daycare waiting for you to pick me up while you're too wrecked to remember me. I don't need you to keep your job so I can eat dinner. You're not my role model on how to go through life.

KITTY. *(Tightly.)* I would've been clean.

B. Okay. Let's play this game. Yes! You would've been clean.

KITTY. Would it kill you to believe me for once?

B. I don't understand how you can say that this – it – would be so important to you but be ready to risk its well-being by taking a gamble – because it's a gamble, Kitty, it's not a set deal – and say to my face you'll like, oh, I dunno, probably, maybe, hopefully stay clean.

KITTY. It doesn't have to be a gamble.

B. I know you have this nice idealistic view that once you quit you're done forever but I can promise you that's nobody. That wasn't me, that wasn't anyone I knew, that's not you.

KITTY. Maybe I have more willpower.

B. Right.

KITTY. Maybe I'm more motivated. Maybe for a kid I'd –

B. "Maybe" being the operative word. Or maybe you'd end up with this thing you thought you wanted only to find that taking care of it and not using is actually really, really hard.

KITTY. This thing I thought I wanted.

B. Well, didn't you?

KITTY. Didn't you?

B. What I want is to – I don't know. See you happy, before you implode on me or disappear. Because I like you. I do – I really like you, Kitty.

KITTY. I'm not a time bomb.

(He's unconvinced.)

I'm not! I can get it together whenever I want to.

B. We were almost talking.

KITTY. "Talking" is a discussion. Talking isn't you *lecturing* me on how I'm going to explode or –

B. *(Correcting her.) Im*plode.

KITTY. *Im*plode as though I'm not even here, as though I'm not even a person, as –

B. That isn't what I said at all. You know that isn't what I said. Christ Kitty, don't be stupid.

KITTY. I'm not stupid! You think that I'm stupid because I didn't graduate but I'm not! I'm not!

B. No, I think you're stupid because you think having a kid when you're always half-wrecked is smart. And because you're being completely illogical – and you smoke crack.

KITTY. *I'm not stupid!*

B. *(Brusque.)* Well that just happens to be my personal definition. But don't worry. It's sort of endearing.

(Silence.)

Kitty, I –

KITTY. Stop.

B. I'm sorry. I shouldn't've –

KITTY. No, listen to me. Stop. I mean it. I mean, stop.

B. I'm stopping.

KITTY. That was…

B. Cruel.

KITTY. *(Finishing her own sentence.)* Small.

(Silence again.)

B. You know what? You should be sitting. Or – resting. We shouldn't… It's fine. We don't need to talk about this anymore.

KITTY. You think we don't need to talk about this anymore.

B. It's upsetting you and I don't want to and –
KITTY. Upsetting me.
B. Yes.
KITTY. Upsetting me.
B. Yes, Kitty.
KITTY. Do you want to talk about what's upsetting me? I know you're torturing yourself or something because you think you pushed me into something I didn't want and maybe that's true but at the end of the day *I* made a choice, *I* did it. How can you say I'm stupid for a habit I'm kicking, or for having a kid I didn't even have? I didn't have it. I know that we're broke and that it wouldn't have worked. You made compelling arguments. I listened. I'm not upset that I did what I did – I'm upset that I had to. Because we *are* broke and that it *wouldn't* have worked.
B. Well you know what, you don't get to complain about being broke when you spend half your income on –
KITTY. Don't. Even. You spend half *your* income on Nirvana CDs.
B. CDs which incidentally do not kill you, and are not sold by people who could kill you, or rape you, or –
KITTY. I don't know, that shop around the corner is pretty sketchy if you ask me.
B. *(Dry.)* Ha ha.

(Beat.)

KITTY. And I'm upset because of the whiplash, I think?
B. Whiplash. You're one to talk.
KITTY. You carried me into our room.

(Beat.)

Afterwards. Or did you already forget? You picked me up from Planned Parenthood and we got to our door and you lifted me up like something you cared about and carried me into our room. *(She smiles.)* You offered me your headphones and your music.
B. You weren't really awake.

KITTY. I was awake. You walked slowly. Like you didn't want to jostle me, or something.

B. They said you weren't supposed to be on your feet, so.

KITTY. You laid me on our bed. Kissed my forehead. Said, "Everything's going to be okay, sweetheart." *(Beat.)* And now I'm stupid, right? How does that work?

(**B** *starts to answer, but can't.*)

This whole week we haven't spoken. You make me Ramen and set it on the bedside table, don't say a word. I call your name, you come in with painkillers, ask dully if I need another blanket. Maybe ask how I'm feeling like it's a chore. Don't look at my face. *(Pause.)* Why? Why do I have to be just entertaining? Why do we have to just be having fun – nothing too serious… Why can't we always be the kind of people who carry each other to bedrooms and promise that things happen for a reason?

B. Because if you aren't just entertaining, because if you are… *(Struggling)* …important to me, and Kitty you *are* important to me, what happens next if you overdose or get killed or do something stupid? What happens to me? You think you're invincible or something?

KITTY. I don't think I'm invincible! You don't factor in how much I want it.

B. Oh, how much you want it?

KITTY. Us. You don't factor it in!

B. Well you don't get "us" when you're ten feet off the ground whenever I'm not in the room, you don't get both, you –

KITTY. *You* don't take into account that I want us, and a desk job, and a GED and to live by the beach and to amount to something – to be responsible – you don't know I want it!

B. You want it.

KITTY. I want it. *(Beat.)* Baby? I want to do it. I'm ready.

B. *(Somewhat unconvinced.)* Ready.

KITTY. When I do the shit I do I get to be anything. You know? I get to be infinite. Ten feet off the ground and I don't have stringy hair or a shit job – I can be a princess or a fairy or a bird. One time I was so convinced I really was a daisy. Don't you remember? I could feel it. I don't have all *this*. I don't have to be just *this*. But you – you make "this" worth it, okay? You make it seem impermanent – you make solid ground worth it and surviving this mess worth it because maybe if I get there eventually I can be more. I promise, it's worth it. You make it worth it. I want this.

B. Only this.

KITTY. Only this.

(A pause.)

B. Kitty? About your pulse?

KITTY. Mm?

B. It doesn't thud.

KITTY. What?

B. You said it thuds. It doesn't.

KITTY. I think I would know…

B. It's too frantic to thud. And too explosive. You know?

KITTY. Explosive.

B. Like a thud, that's dread. Or a tree falling. I don't think yours is like that. Yours is like life.

KITTY. Yours is like home.

(A pause.)

Are you sure it sounds that way? Like life?

B. I'm sure.

KITTY. How do you know?

B. Because I'm listening now.

KITTY. Are you really?

B. I promise.

(She smiles.)

KITTY. I'm glad.

End of Play

This Play is About Pirates

by

Caleigh Derreberry

THIS PLAY IS ABOUT PIRATES was presented in a staged reading as part of the Thespian Playworks program at the 2014 Thespian Festival on June 28. Phillip Moss was director, Nicholas C. Pappas served as dramaturg, and Samantha Allen served as stage manager. The cast was as follows:

JIM	Liam Myhill
JAMES	Joe Bills
MARY	Kelsey Reese
MAD PETE	Trenton Kerger
WIDOWIN' WALLACE	Megan Walker
PIRATES	Connor Hamilton, Jorge Zamora, Nate Womak, Mary Ellen Cobb

ABOUT THE PLAYWRIGHT

Caleigh Derreberry is a freshman at Georgia Institute of Technology where she studies Literature, Media, and Communications. Her work has been honored by the Southeastern Theatre Conference, Rockford New Play Festival, Young Voices with New Vision Contest, and the Scholastic Art & Writing Awards. She aspires to be a screenwriter/playwright. She would like to thank Nick Pappas and Phillip Moss for helping to shape *Pirates* into what it is today.

CHARACTERS

JIM – A pirate; three years older than James
JAMES – A memory; three years younger than Jim
MARY – His lover
MAD PETE – Her father, a pirate
WIDOWIN' WALLACE – A pirate, a lover, a pain
PAT – A pirate with a limited vocabulary
SULLY – A pirate with limited patience

SETTING

A bare stage except for two benches placed stage right and stage left. On top of one of the benches is a treasure chest with "MACGUFFIN'S NECKLACE" written across it in large letters. Jim sits on the other bench. Most of the scenes occur in the space between the two benches. NOTE: Jim is never in the dark unless otherwise indicated.

(Dramatic red lights. **SULLY** *and* **PAT** *are on stage singing a song similar to the* Pirates of the Caribbean *theme. They don't have to be very good.* **JIM** *enters, crossing in front of the two pirates. He wears ridiculous pirate dress-up clothes – hat, red-striped shirt, long coat – but he carries a very real sword. When he talks, it's with an exaggerated pirate accent, though he frequently drops it.)*

JIM. *(To audience.)* Theatre is the art of memories. *(Snorts.)* That's the sort of bullcrap ye can expect from this here play. *(To* **SULLY** *and* **PAT**.) Stop singing, ye nit wits! Oye, Sully, fix the lights why don't ye? And ye – ye know what to do.

PAT. *(Yeah, yeah.)* Arrrggghh.

*(***SULLY** *and* **PAT** *exit and the lights change.* **JIM** *sits on one of the benches.)*

JIM. *(To audience.)* I'd leave if I were you. This ain't a good play. I remember when I came to see it, 'bout three years ago – and look what happened, I got stuck here! *(Points to* **JAMES**, *who is sitting in the audience.)* That's me in the back. The funny-lookin' one in the striped shirt.

*(***JAMES** *wears the same shirt as* **JIM**. *He stands up and looks around awkwardly.)*

Come on up here, I need ye.

*(***JAMES**, *confused but excited, makes his way up to the stage as* **JIM** *narrates.)*

(To audience.) I'ma tell ye the story of how a sissy lad like him became the most feared pirate cap'n in the Midwest. It ain't a pretty story, but at least it gots a few good fights in it. I'll start at the beginning. Once erpon a time, I was born in Okleehomey –

> (**JAMES** *gets onstage and excitedly holds his hand out for* **JIM** *to shake.*)

JAMES. This is such an honor to meet you – me – us. I can't believe I become a pirate! Have you met Mad Pete? Or Widowin' –

JIM. *(Standing up and brandishing his sword.)* You'll shut up and let me tell me story if you want to keep that pretty face of yers.

> (**JAMES** *retracts his hand.*)

JAMES. Sorry.

> (**JIM** *drops his sword and offers his hand to* **JAMES**.)

JIM. Me name's Jim. Cap'n Jim, most feared pirate captain in the Midwest.

JAMES. *(Shaking his hand.)* James.

JIM. Sissy name, James.

> (**JIM** *sits down.* **JAMES**, *much to* **JIM**'s *annoyance, sits beside him.*)

JAMES. It's a family name – but you know that. My aunt says my great-grandfather –

JIM. I said shut up! *(Beat.)* Now where was I?

JAMES. You were talking about how you – me – us became the most feared pirate in all of the Midwest.

JIM. Right, right. *(To audience.)* Let me just skip to the good part. The part where I stop being so annoyin' and learn to man up. Ye see, one day I saw this lass I worked with gettin' beat up.

> (**MARY** *runs onstage. She is beautiful but plain. She trips.*)

JAMES. Mary?

JIM. Aye. She sure is a beauty.

JAMES. I'll say. Those eyes.

JIM. That booty.

> (**SULLY** *and* **PAT** *enter. They make large swooping motions with their swords.*)

SULLY. Give us all ye booty!

PAT. Arrrggghh!

(They just kick her.)

JIM. *(To* **JAMES.***)* Go on – help her!

*(***JAMES*** runs over to the two pirates and balls his fists in an attempt to look menacing.)*

JAMES. *(Half-heartedly.)* Arrgh?

*(***SULLY*** and* **PAT*** laugh menacingly.)*

JIM. *(To* **SULLY** *and* **PAT.***)* That's yer cue to leave.

SULLY. Yeah, yeah, we know.

PAT. *(Yeah, yeah, we know.)* Arrrggghh.

*(***SULLY*** and* **PAT*** exit.* **JAMES*** bends down to help* **MARY.***)*

JAMES. Are you OK?

MARY. No, I think I sprained my ankle. And my shoulder's bleeding. And I'm on my period.

JAMES. Oh. OK, well I have to help you. I'll take you to a doctor.

(He picks her up like a groom carrying his bride over the threshold.)

Did those guys look like pirates to you?

MARY. *(Nervous.)* No. Definitely not pirates. Maybe the circus. Or a gang. Or drugs. Not pirates though.

(She purposefully falls out of **JAMES***'s arms.)*

Ow! Doctor! I need a doctor!

*(***JAMES*** picks her up again and exits. Center stage blackout.)*

JIM. Lookie, I know this ain't exactly the most exciting part of the play, but I promise ye there'll be action and fighting later on. We just got to get through these stupid love scenes first.

(Center stage lights up. **MARY** *and* **JAMES** *are lying asleep onstage.)*

I remember this. I stayed in the hospital with her all night. *(To stage crew.)* Oye, Sully, wake 'em up, will ye! People didn't pay money to watch 'em sleep.

*(**SULLY** enters.)*

SULLY. *(Gently.)* Oye, Mary, time to get up lass, come on.

*(**SULLY** hits **JAMES** on the head.)*

Get up ye scallywag!

JAMES. Wha – *(Seeing **MARY**.)* Oh! You're awake. I mean – *(voice drops an octave)* – you're awake.

MARY. Yep.

JAMES. Are you OK? It's not every day you get attacked by pirates.

MARY. *(Too forcefully.)* They weren't pirates.

JAMES. Are you sure? They had swords.

MARY. My ex-boyfriend works at Medieval Times.

JAMES. Oh.

(Awkward pause.)

I'm James.

MARY. Mary.

JAMES. I know. We work in the same building. I'm on the third floor. Accounting.

MARY. Right.

(Another awkward pause.)

JIM. Yawn! Lemme give ye the SparkNotes version. It be a truth universally acknowledged that a hot single lass will fall in love with ye if ye save her life.

*(**JAMES** and **MARY** kiss. It is awkward but sweet. They pull apart, then begin passionately making out.)*

Why do you think I stayed with her all night?

*(**MARY** suddenly stops the kiss.)*

MARY. Pirates! They were pirates!

JAMES. Yes, I knew it!

*(He leans in for another kiss and remains in the same position, oblivious to what **MARY** says, until **MARY** slaps him.)*

MARY. My dad's a pirate.
JAMES. Gotcha
MARY. A real, bloodthirsty pirate.
JAMES. Cool.
MARY. He uses swords and cannons and everything
JAMES. Can I see your treasure chests?

(**MARY** *slaps him.*)

MARY. This isn't a game.
JAMES. Jesus Mary, I know that. You didn't have to slap me.
MARY. PIRATES! MY DAD IS A PIRATE!
JAMES. Yeah, that's awesome! I love pirates! My aunt used to tell me stories about the epic rivalry between –
MARY. A real, ruthless pirate. He's not like Captain Hook or Jack Sparrow or any of the pirates you see on TV. Sure, he wears the same stupid outfits and they still say "arrgghhh" and drink too much, but they kill people. He kills people.
JAMES. *(Taking* **MARY***'s hand.)* I'm OK with that. Just don't slap me again.

(Center stage blackout. **SULLY** *and* **PAT** *enter carrying a bench.)*

JIM. What ye got that fer?
SULLY. It's fer the scene, the one where ye propose to Mary –
JIM. Shut up befer ye spoil the show! I haven't even met the lass's father yet.
SULLY. *(Mumbling.)* I knew I should've taken that Penzance job.
PAT. *(Mumbling.)* Arrrgggh.

(**SULLY** *and* **PAT** *exit with the bench.*)

JIM. Now, where was I?

(**MAD PETE** *ARRRGGHHHs offstage.*)

Oh, right. Her father.

(Lights up on **MARY** *and* **JAMES** *center stage.* **JAMES** *paces.)*

JAMES. *(Excited.)* I can't believe I'm going to meet the Mad Pete. I grew up hearing stories about his never-ending conflict with the evil Widowin' Wallace and how he plundered the sea chasing the evil Bloody Burt.

MARY. *(Mumbling.)* Actually, that was just my science teacher who gave me a C.

JAMES. This is a bad idea.

(**MARY** *embraces* **JAMES** *in an attempt to comfort him.*)

MARY. You're right.

JAMES. I'm right? Don't tell me I'm right!

MARY. What do you want me to tell you? That you have nothing to worry about?

JAMES. Yes!

MARY. You don't have anything to worry about. You're just meeting an insane pirate captain.

JAMES. What if he doesn't like me?

MARY. That's what you're worried about? That he won't like you?

JAMES. Yeah.

MARY. He's killed people!

JAMES. People he didn't like.

(*Threatening noises from offstage: a door slams, feet stomp, a loud "ARRGGHHH!"*)

(Fixing his hair.) Do I look OK?

MAD PETE. *(Offstage.)* I'M GONNA KILL THAT MOTHER ARRGER. HE CAN'T TAKE ME DAUGHTER AND GET AWAY WITH IT, THE SON OF AN ARRGGGHHH.

JIM. I had to censor him.

(**MAD PETE** *enters. He's your stereotypical pirate – eyepatch, sword, bad accent. As the name implies, he is completely mad.* **JAMES** *attempts to shake his hand, but* **MARY** *quickly shoves in front of him, positioning herself between the two men.*)

MAD PETE. Move, Mary. Let the piece of ARRGGHH face me like a man.

(He draws his sword. **JAMES** *tries to push past* **MARY**, *but she doesn't budge.)*

MARY. You promised no swords!

*(***MAD PETE** *reluctantly lowers his sword.* **MARY** *grabs* **JAMES***'s hand and shoves it towards her father to shake.)*

Dad, this is my boyfriend, James.

MAD PETE. *(Sneering.)* Stupid name.

*(***JIM** *scoffs in agreement.)*

MARY. He's an accountant that works in my building. We've been dating for almost three months now. He knows that you're a ruthless pirate captain who could kill him with a single blow.

MAD PETE. *(Mumbling, flattered.)* He's right.

MARY. But even though he's scared of you – like everyone should be scared of you – he still agreed to meet you because he knew it would make me happy.

(She yanks **JAMES***'s hand even more roughly towards her father. An order.)*

Don't. Hurt. Him.

*(***MAD PETE** *mumbles in affirmation and reluctantly shakes* **JAMES***'s hand. As they shake,* **JAMES** *becomes very enthusiastic. He pushes past* **MARY** *so he's standing face to face with her father.)*

JAMES. I'm a big fan of your work, sir. I think you're the scariest pirate captain in all of the Midwest. My aunt used to tell me bedtime stories about the epic rivalry between you and Widowin' Wallace. You were clearly the better pirate, sir.

MAD PETE. *(Confused – but enjoying this.)* Thanks. Always nice to meet a fan.

JAMES. Actually, I was wondering if you had any job openings?

MAD PETE. Huh?

JAMES. I wanna work for you. On your ship.

MAD PETE. There be no need for an accountant on a pirate ship, lad.

JAMES. I don't want a job as an accountant. I want to be part of the crew.

(**MAD PETE** *starts to laugh like a madman.*)

MAD PETE. That be a good one. *(To* **MARY**.*)* Ye got yerself a regular ol' jokester.

MARY. Yeah, good joke, James.

JAMES. I'm not kidding.

(**MAD PETE** *abruptly stops laughing.*)

MARY. *(Devastated.)* What?

MAD PETE. You lil' motherarrger. It be one thing to think yer good enough fer me only daughter, but ye ain't even almost arrging good enough to get anywhere near me ship.

JAMES. I'm a hard worker.

MAD PETE. You'd be sleeping with the sharks by lunch.

JAMES. I've had all of my shots.

MAD PETE. That is, if the crew didn't eat you fer breakfast.

JAMES. I made a 1900 on the SAT.

MAD PETE. Ye'd make me the laughing stock of Oklahoma.

JAMES. I'm the Miltonville County hotdog eating champion.

MAD PETE. *(Devious.)* Fine – I'll make ye a deal.

(**MAD PETE** *pulls a map out of his jacket. He unfolds it and unfolds it and unfolds it and unfolds it. The map is comically large with "IT'S ON THE BENCH" written on it in large letters, though this is not explicitly shown to the audience.*)

See, me and Widowin' Wallace have this lil' bet going about who can find MacGuffin's necklace first.

JAMES. MacGuffin's necklace?

MAD PETE. It's old and valuable and ugly. You find it fer me before Wallace does, I'll *(swallowing his displeasure)* let ye aboard me ship.

JAMES. Thank you!

MARY. And if Wallace finds it first?

MAD PETE. Well, Wallace don't have the map so ye don't got anything to worry 'bout – other then the fact that yer racing against a cutthroat pirate who will kill ye if they even knew ye wanted that necklace. And lots of people have died looking for that treasure. And I hate ye.

JAMES. But if I find it, I can be a pirate, right?

MAD PETE. *(Affirmative.)* Arrrggghhhh.

JAMES. Thank you, sir!

(JAMES *hugs* MAD PETE.)

MAD PETE. Watch the sword.

(He growls and exits.)

JAMES. *(Attempting to read the map.)* Am I holding this thing correctly?

(MARY *slaps* JAMES.)

(Confused.) You said you wouldn't do that anymore!

MARY. You can't be a pirate!

JAMES. Why not?

MARY. You just can't!

JAMES. If I can figure out this map I can.

MARY. You can't just leave your life here to tramp around the world and steal treasure from people.

JAMES. Yes, I can. It's not a big deal. Definitely not something to get mad about.

MARY. I'm not mad!

JAMES. Good! Because you're my girlfriend and you're supposed to support me. And you know how to read maps.

MARY. *(Gesturing to the map.)* Just give that to me.

(He hands her the map.)

JAMES. Promise you aren't mad?

MARY. I'm not mad! Come on. We need to go this way.

(They exit. Center stage blackout.)

JIM. Lemme tell ye, Mad Pete is one crazy mother-arrging pirate. MacGuffin's necklace is near impossible to find. Sneaky bastard, giving it to me when I was still green. Neither he nor his crew could find it, but he expected me to –

*(**MARY** sneaks into **JIM**'s light carrying the map. She is oblivious to **JIM**, but **JIM** can clearly see her.)*

JIM. *(Sans accent.)* Hey, you're interrupting my narration!

*(**MARY**, surprised, attempts to hide the comically large map behind her back.)*

MARY. Sorry! I didn't know anybody was out here. Guess I'll just be leaving then.

*(**JIM** grabs her wrists. She struggles but can't break free.)*

Let go of me!

JIM. I remember what yer doing. Ye can't stop James from becoming a pirate.

MARY. You don't know that.

JIM. I think I do.

MARY. The future's not set.

JIM. That might be true. But I ain't the future, yer just the past, and I think that proves I know what I'm talking about.

MARY. *(Struggling.)* Let go of me!

JIM. Tell me why James getting what he wants is such a bad thing.

MARY. Let me go!

JIM. Tell me!

*(She stops struggling and looks at **JIM**. They are standing so close they could be kissing.)*

MARY. Pirates are bad people. Lonely people. He'll just end up sitting alone on a bare stage.

JIM. *(Sans accent.)* That's a very, very good reason. *(Pause. **JIM** resumes the accent.)* Unfortunately, I'ma have to tell him about anything suspicious I see.

MARY. Please –

JIM. Of course, if I don't see nothing…

*(**JIM** covers his eyes with his hand and turns his back to **MARY**. **MARY** crosses to the treasure chest, opens it, and takes the necklace out.)*

MARY. Thank you.

(**JAMES** *uncovers his eyes. Smiles at her. She exits.* **SULLY** *and* **PAT** *enter with the bench.*)

JIM. *(Sans accent.)* No, it's not time for that! I still have a few scenes left!

SULLY. Well, see we was thinkin' ye might cud do this scene a lil' earlier tonight. We figure it's the only scene ye want t'do anyway and it don't ev'r change much, and Pat here pirated a copy o' *Wizard o' Oz* we wanted t' watch.

PAT. *(Excited.)* Arrrggghh!

JIM. *(With accent.)* That sounds an awful lot like mutiny to me.

SULLY. It's not mutiny, it's a classic.

JIM. It ain't time for this scene!

(**SULLY** *and* **PAT** *exit.*)

(To audience.) Anyway, where was I?

(From offstage we hear…something. It might be someone saying "ARRRRGGGHH.")

Oh, right, we was lookin' fer MacGuffin's necklace.

(Center stage lights up. **MARY** *and* **JAMES** *enter.* **MARY** *is reading the map.* **JAMES** *is making AARRRRGGGHHHH noises, but he sounds more like a car or an animal than a pirate.)*

MARY. What are you doing?

JAMES. Just trying to find my *(low, unrecognizable)* arrrrggg.

MARY. Your what?

JAMES. Aaaaaaarr.

MARY. What?

JAMES. A-R-R-R-G-H. For when I'm a pirate

MARY. Could you find it a little quieter?

JAMES. Pirates aren't quiet.

(**MARY** *gives him a look.*)

I'll be quiet.

(From offstage we hear a loud, distinct ARRRGGHHHH.)

MARY. I thought I said –

(**WIDOWIN' WALLACE** *enters, flanked by* **SULLY** *and* **PAT**. *She is beautiful but terrifying. Exotic, articulate, dignified – and completely insane. Ideally, she is of a different ethnicity than* **MARY**.)

JIM. Now that's the kind of booty I'd like to plunder.

WALLACE. Well, well, well. What lovely visitors. Mad Pete's daughter and – *(To* **JAMES**.*)* Who are you?

JAMES. *(At a loss.)* James?

WALLACE. How droll. You look more like a Jim to me.

MARY. What do you want, Wallace?

JAMES. *(Excited.)* Widowin' Wallace? You're Widowin' Wallace? But you're a girl!

SULLY. Not t' smartest thin' t' say t' Widowin' Wallace, lad.

(**WALLACE** *draws her sword.*)

WALLACE. Your point is?

PAT. *(Really? You went for that pun?)* Arrrrgghh.

JAMES. Nothing. I love girls. I just didn't realize Widowin' Wallace was a girl. But that's good. Girls are good.

(**WALLACE** *walks threateningly toward* **JAMES**. *She kisses him.*)

MARY. Stop!

(Beat. **WALLACE** *doesn't stop.)*

That's my boyfriend!

(Beat.)

We have the map!

(Beat.)

The map to MacGuffin's necklace, we have it!

(**WALLACE** *stops.*)

WALLACE. How fascinating! Give it to me.

JAMES. But I need that!

WALLACE. Oh? Do explain.

JAMES. Mad Pete said I can join his crew if I find that necklace.

WALLACE. *(As if it's Christmas.)* So you want to be a pirate?
JAMES. Yes.
SULLY. Not t' smartest thin' t' say t' Widowin' Wallace, lad.
WALLACE. *(To pirates.)* He wants to be a pirate, isn't that grand?

(Overlapping:)

SULLY. Well the pay ain't all that good.
PAT. *(That's not grand.)* Arrrgggh.
WALLACE. *(Crazier.)* That is grand, isn't it?

(Overlapping:)

SULLY. Yep, very grand, good career choice.
PAT. *(Falsely enthusiastic.)* Arrrgggghhh!
WALLACE. *(To JAMES.)* I can mold you into a pirate.
JAMES. Really?

(WALLACE grabs JAMES by the arm and pulls him downstage.)

WALLACE. I'll teach you how to read the stars and to know your location just by the color of the sea. You'll crisscross the map so many times your footprints will overlap and the locals will know you by the sound of your boots and give you a terrifying pirate name.
JAMES. Like Jailbird James.
WALLACE. More like Jim.
JAMES. Oh.
WALLACE. One day you'll understand the thrill of chasing a treasure forgotten by time as you watch your hands splinter and your eyes dull from exposure to the sun. And you'll never regret any of it. Because it's all worth it if it means you can fall asleep to the song of the sea and wake up to the cooing of seagulls.
JAMES. Yes!
WALLACE. I'll show you that life on the ocean is more liberating than any life you'll have on land. But before that – before the stars and the ocean and the freedom – I'll show you what a real pirate acts like.

(**WALLACE** *quickly turns and traps* **MARY** *in a chokehold.*)

JAMES. Stop!

WALLACE. No. Baby, you will learn how cruel this wonderful world is if it's the last thing I do. Bring me that necklace or she will crisscross the world and leave a limb in each of its corners.

JAMES. If I bring it to you, you'll leave her alone? And you'll teach me all those things?

WALLACE. Of course.

JAMES. *(A little too eager.)* I'll do it.

WALLACE. *(To* **MARY.***)* Give him the map.

(She does.)

MARY. What? James –

JAMES. Everything will be OK. I'll find her necklace and I'll rescue you. After all, all I have to do is follow the map.

(Her hand goes to her neck, where she has hidden the necklace.)

MARY. *(Hesitantly.)* Good luck.

JAMES. Don't worry, I'll be fine.

(He leans in to kiss her and **WALLACE** *yanks her back.* **JAMES** *and* **MARY** *settle for a handshake.)*

See you soon. *(He exits.)*

WALLACE. I think I like that kid. *(To* **MARY.***)* Can you give me his number?

(Center stage blackout. **JAMES** *enters humming the song from the beginning and following the map about the stage. He runs into* **JIM.***)*

JAMES. Oh – sorry!

JIM. Ye know yer holding that thing upside down.

*(***JAMES** *flips the map the correct way.)*

JAMES. Oh – that makes more sense.

(He sits down beside **JIM,** *much to* **JIM***'s annoyance.)*

I'm really bad at this.

JIM. Yeah, ye are. Don't worry, ye get better.

JAMES. Do you like it?

JIM. What?

JAMES. Being a pirate.

JIM. Don't be a ninny, o'course I do.

JAMES. I just mean – is it everything we dreamed about?

JIM. Don't ye have a necklace to find?

JAMES. Do you get to crisscross maps?

JIM. Lots o'em.

JAMES. Are there sword fights?

JIM. Sometimes.

JAMES. And treasure! Do you find lots of treasure?

JIM. I find enough.

JAMES. Wow. That sounds incredible. You must be so happy.

(Beat.)

JIM. Here, lad, I got something fer ye – to help ye with yer journey. It's captured maidens, slayed dreams, and inspired fear in the hearts of sailors for centuries.

(He takes out a small box – to everyone but **JAMES**, *it is obviously a jewelry box – and gives it to* **JAMES**. **JAMES** *attempts to open it.* **JIM** *hits him.)*

Don't use it now, ye sissy. Only open it when yer life can't get any worse. It'll fix everythin' fer ye.

JAMES. *(Shakes the box.)* It doesn't sound like much.

JIM. *(Annoyed.)* Aren't ye supposed to be lookin' fer somethin'?

JAMES. Oh. Right. *(He looks at the map.)* You haven't seen MacGuffin's necklace, recently, have you?

JIM. I ain't seen nothing.

JAMES. Oh.

*(***JAMES** *looks at the map, obviously still confused.)*

JIM. *(Pointing in the direction of the treasure chest.)* It be that way.

*(***JAMES** *follows the map to the treasure chest. He opens it.)*

JAMES. Wha – No! It has to be here!

(He slams the treasure chest and collapses to the floor.)

JIM. *(To audience.)* Lil' bit of a drama queen, wouldn't ye say? Mary! Wallace! Get out here! Sully, Pat, yer on cleanup duty.

(WALLACE and MARY enter as SULLY and PAT carry JAMES to center stage. MARY runs over to JAMES and sits on the floor beside him, holding his hand. He is still unconscious. WALLACE kicks him. He comes to, and only sees MARY.)

JAMES. *(Longingly.)* Mary.

(WALLACE crouches on the other side of him.)

WALLACE. ARRGGHHHH.

(JAMES jumps back. WALLACE laughs. She holds her hand expectantly out to JAMES.)

The necklace. *(Beat.)* Now.

JAMES. *(A fact.)* No.

WALLACE. How exceptionally pirate of you. Give me the necklace.

JAMES. No.

WALLACE. *(Jabbing her sword toward his face.)* I don't see the point in all this arguing.

PAT. *(Really? Again?)* Arrrrrrgggh.

MARY. You already made that joke.

(JAMES takes the box JIM gave him out of his pocket and holds it out as protection.)

JAMES. Don't make me use this.

WALLACE. Please. You don't want to use that on me.

MARY. Don't touch him.

SULLY. Here, lass, ye might need this.

(SULLY throws MARY his sword. WALLACE and MARY duel.)

WALLACE. I don't think you've grasped my point yet.

PAT. *(Seriously?)* Arrrggghh.

(MARY *knocks* WALLACE*'s sword out of her hand and sucker-punches her in the gut.*)

MARY. Get a new punchline.

JAMES. I love you.

(MARY*'s hand goes to her neck, where the necklace is still hidden.*)

MARY. Don't forget that.

(*Center stage blackout.*)

JIM. Can you believe I bought that bull crap? (*Mocking.*) Don't forget that – who says things like that?

(SULLY *enters.*)

SULLY. Ye need t' get on with t' story. Some of us ain't got time fer yer commentary.

JIM. (*Rolling his eyes.*) ARRGGHHH

(SULLY *exits.*)

Here ye go, another scene. As requested.

(*Center stage lights up.* MAD PETE *sits on the center stage bench.* JAMES *and* MARY *stand in front of him.*)

MAD PETE. I was right about ye from the beginning, boy.

JAMES. (*Half-heartedly.*) Arrggghhh.

MAD PETE. Don't say Arrgghh! Say 'No' like a normal person! Ye ain't no pirate, lad. Yer n'vr gonna be one.

(JIM *coughs.*)

JAMES. You're right.

(JIM *coughs even louder.*)

MAD PETE. (*Surprised.*) Oh – well, good! Don't let me see yer grubby face ever again!

MARY. He's coming over for Thanksgiving.

MAD PETE. Well, don't let me see yer grubby face – until Thanksgiving!

(JAMES *and* MARY *begin to exit.*)

(*Sneering at the idea.*) You, a pirate! Ye woulda dried up in the heat befer we even got out to sea. Probably woulda called ye something like Jumpy Jim.

JAMES. James.

MAD PETE. Or Juvenile Jim. Or Jiggly Jim.

JIM. (*To audience.*) Actually, they call me the Jim Reaper. Captain Jim Reaper.

MAD PETE. I should make ye walk the plank fer even thinking ye could get on me ship.

(**JAMES** *turns to exit.* **MARY** *stays.*)

MARY. I won't let him end up like M – (*She starts to say "Mom," then stops herself.*) Jack.

MAD PETE. Jack?

MARY. The dachshund I had when I was a kid.

MAD PETE. The one that died?

MARY. The one that was killed. Remember? One of your pirates thought it'd be funny to see if he could swim.

MAD PETE. I'm sorry.

MARY. You're not.

MAD PETE. I got ye another dog.

MARY. You couldn't get me another mother!

MAD PETE. (*Sorry, but not regretful.*) Arrgghhh.

(*Beat. She shows him the necklace.*)

He said he didn't find it the – arrging – Pirate!

MARY. He's not a liar.

MAD PETE. (*Understanding.*) Oh. He don't know.

(*He reaches for the necklace, but* **MARY** *pulls it away.*)

MARY. You keep your pirates far away from my boyfriend and you can have the necklace when this is all over, deal?

MAD PETE. Fine.

MARY. Don't you dare tell him I have it.

MAD PETE. I won't. I'm proud of ye.

(**MARY** *rushes offstage.*)

Oye, Pat, get in here!

(**PAT** *enters.*)

PAT. *(Yes captain?)* Arrrgghhhhhhhh.
MAD PETE. I want ye to write a letter.
PAT. *(Why?)* Arrrgghhhhhhhh?
MAD PETE. It's fer Widowin' Wallace.

(**PAT** *takes out a piece of old parchment paper. Alternatively, this can be done on the back of the map.*)

Start it "ARRGGGGHHHH."

(*Center stage blackout.* **JAMES** *sneaks onstage and begins to open the box.*)

JIM. I told ye not to do that.
JAMES. I need help.
JIM. Ye couldn't find a necklace. That don't mean yer life's bad enough to open that yet.

(**JAMES** *rolls his eyes and opens the box anyway. The only thing inside is a wedding ring.*)

JAMES. A wedding band? A ring is supposed to save my life?
JIM. Ye thought a necklace would.
JAMES. I can't marry Mary.
JIM. Why not?
JAMES. Her father hates me for one thing!
JIM. He hates everybody.
JAMES. I'm in between jobs.
JIM. She ain't marrying ye fer yer job.
JAMES. And I want to be a pirate!
JIM. I didn't ask ye what ye wanted!
JAMES. Why do I have to do this now?
JIM. Why not?
JAMES. That's not a reason.
JIM. Stop making excuses!
JAMES. I don't want to rush into something like this.
JIM. Ye ain't rushin' into anything.
JAMES. We've only been together for three months.
JIM. But ye love her!

JAMES. Yeah, So?

JIM. So marry her!

JAMES. I'm not ready for this! ARRGGGHHH!

JIM. *(Sans accent.)* Don't let go of Mary.

(**JAMES** *nods, puts the ring in his pocket, and exits.*)

(With accent.) Stubborn bastard.

(**JIM** *doesn't look satisfied with this.* **WIDOWIN' WALLACE** *enters.*)

WALLACE. Oye! Jim Reaper.

(He grunts.)

Stop looking so melancholy and greet me properly.

JIM. *(Grunting.)* Wallace. What brings ye to these parts?

WALLACE. Business.

JIM. *(Playing along.)* Ye sure ye don't want to take a break to relax?

WALLACE. Are you flirting with me?

JIM. *(Thrown off.)* Yes?

WALLACE. You're exceptionally bad at it. *(Seductively.)* Maybe you'll be bad at some other things, too.

(He smiles. She sits down beside him.)

JIM. What do ye want?

WALLACE. Mad Pete's daughter.

JIM. *(Defensive, no accent.)* Why?

WALLACE. Relax, Jim. I don't want to hurt her; I know how much she means to you.

JIM. *(With accent.)* Meant. How much she meant to me. In the past. Not now.

WALLACE. Whatever. All I want is MacGuffin's necklace, which her father tells me she possesses. I won't harm the girl.

JIM. I might could help ye then. I happen to know that a certain starry-eyed fool –

WALLACE. You.

JIM. – is going to pop a certain question on a certain center stage bench later.

WALLACE. Marriage, huh? You always were a hopeless romantic. Thanks.

(WALLACE exits.)

JIM. MARY! MARY YOU MISSED YOUR CUE!

MARY. *(Rushing onstage.)* No, not at all – wait, this isn't my scene! You lied to me!

JIM. Wallace knows ye have MacGuffin's necklace.

MARY. What! Did you tell her?

JIM. No!

(MARY isn't convinced.)

Why would I be warning ye if I told her in the first place?

MARY. You're a pirate.

JIM. *(Without accent.)* Just be prepared!

(MARY exits.)

(With accent.) Stubborn bastard.

(Center stage lights up. SULLY and PAT enter with the bench.)

SULLY. It be time, Jim.

JIM. I know.

PAT. *(Sorry.)* Arrrrrggghh.

(SULLY and PAT exit. MARY enters carrying a backpack with two swords obviously in it.)

JIM. Oh. This scene.

JAMES. *(Motioning to her backpack.)* Are those swords?

MARY. No, not at all.

(JAMES nods, distracted.)

JAMES. Will you marry me, Mary?

MARY. What?

JAMES. Oh – the ring! I forgot the ring!

(JAMES gets the ring out and painfully drops to one knee.)

Marry me, Mary!

MARY. What!

JAMES. Someone once told me that my future is better if it's with you. I think I believe that. You've been wonderful and true and honest with me when everything else has been falling apart. And I love you. So – marry me, Mary?!

MARY. Yes!

(They embrace. **WALLACE** *enters, clapping.)*

WALLACE. Oh, how splendorous. Every girl's fantasy!

*(***MARY** *takes out a sword and tosses it to* **JAMES**.*)*

(To **MARY**.*)* You have something I want.

MARY. No I don't.

WALLACE. You don't even know what it is yet.

MARY. But I probably don't have it.

WALLACE. Then tell me exactly what it is I want that you don't have.

MARY. How am I supposed to know? I don't have it.

WALLACE. So you haven't seen MacGuffin's necklace recently?

MARY. No.

WALLACE. Liar.

MARY. I'm no pirate.

WALLACE. Not yet, but you will be. I'm you. From three years in your future.

*(***JAMES** *and* **MARY** *are unimpressed.* **JIM** *snorts.)*

MARY. No you're not.

WALLACE. No I'm not. But I do want that necklace.

MARY. I don't know where it is.

WALLACE. For your sake, Mad Mary, I hope you don't. *(Squeezing* **JAMES**'*s face.)* It'd be a shame if you couldn't recognize such a pretty face in the wedding photos.

MARY. I don't have it.

WALLACE. Don't test me.

JAMES. *(Threatening her with his sword.)* She doesn't have your necklace.

(**WALLACE** *laughs and skillfully brandishes her sword.*)

WALLACE. Baby. You don't want to do this.

(*Beat. They assess each other. It's obvious who the winner of this fight would be.*)

MARY. Here! Have your stupid necklace!

(**MARY** *takes the necklace off and flings it at* **WALLACE**.)

JAMES. Mary?

WALLACE. Nice engagement ring, by the way. You have good taste – (*looking pointedly at* **MARY**) – in jewelry, at least. Call me.

(**WALLACE** *exits. There is silence.*)

MARY. She's right. The ring is nice.

JAMES. I know how much you love your jewelry.

MARY. This was never about the necklace.

JAMES. Then why take it? Did your father tell you to?

MARY. No!

JAMES. Do you want to be a pirate?

MARY. No!

JAMES. So you just wanted to see me fail?

MARY. No!

JAMES. Tell me why you took it!

MARY. I couldn't let you become a pirate.

JAMES. That wasn't your choice to make.

MARY. I'm not sorry I made it.

JAMES. Give me a real answer. Remind me that I love you!

(*Beat.* **JAMES** *begins to exit.*)

MARY. No, don't leave! I love you.

JAMES. Stop lying, Mad Mary.

(**MARY** *runs after him.*)

MARY. I need you, James.

(**JAMES** *angrily turns around. She takes a step back.*)

JAMES. Don't call me that. It's Jim. I'm Jim.

JIM. *(To* **JAMES**. *He talks without an accent and never regains it.)* Stop this, you love her.

JAMES. I want to be a pirate.

*(***JAMES** *starts to walk away.)*

MARY. *(To* **JIM**.*)* You're going to let him leave?

JIM. He's stubborn

*(***MARY** *slaps* **JIM**.*)*

You promised you wouldn't do that.

(They kiss.)

MARY. Please.

JIM. *(To* **JAMES**.*)* Consider what you're doing.

*(***JAMES** *stops and turns around. Considers.)*

JAMES. *(Charging* **JIM**.*)* ARRRRGGGHHHHHHH.

(He knocks **JAMES** *down. They fight, moving around the entire theatre – on the stairs, in the audience. At first they appear evenly matched, but* **JAMES** *begins to get the upper hand.* **JIM** *talks during the whole thing.* **MARY** *watches, unsure of whose side to take.)*

JIM. I told you this wasn't a good play. The characters are clichéd and most of the ongoing jokes aren't even that funny. You probably missed the whole point – it's not a play about love or ambition or destiny or bad pirate puns. It's not even about pirates.

*(***JAMES** *pins* **JIM** *to the ground.)*

At least it's a short play. This is almost the end.

*(***JIM** *laughs.* **MARY** *places herself between* **JIM** *and* **JAMES**, *protecting* **JIM**.*)*

JAMES. Why are you protecting him? He's a pirate – forget about him!

MARY. I will never forget you!

JAMES. *(To* **JIM**.*)* You're fine just being a memory?

JIM. That's all you are. She is.

(Beat. Something shifts.)

JAMES. I need your hat.

(**JIM** *gives it to him.*)

And your jacket.

(**JIM** *gives it to him.*)

And your sword

(**JIM**, *reluctantly, gives it to him. They shake hands.*)

JIM. Good luck.

(**JIM** *and* **MARY** *exit together.* **JAMES** *begins to put on* **JIM**'s *clothes as lights fade to a full blackout. Abrupt dramatic red lights.* **SULLY** *and* **PAT** *are lined up onstage singing a song similar to the* Pirates of the Caribbean *theme.* **JAMES** *enters, wearing* **JIM**'s *clothes. He crosses in front of the line of pirates. This is all very familiar.*)

JAMES. *(To* **SULLY** *and* **PAT**, *with a bad accent.)* Stop!

(**SULLY** *and* **PAT** *stop singing.*)

Theatre is the art of memories.

(He stops. Looks at his sword. Looks at the audience. Considers. Without accent:) I was wrong before. Theatre is not the art of memories. It's the memory of art.

(He runs offstage, exiting in the opposite direction from **JIM** *and* **MARY**. *Blackout.*)

End of Play

Skin

by
Derick Edgren

SKIN was presented in a staged reading as part of the Thespian Playworks program at the 2014 Thespian Festival on June 28, 2014. Elise Kauzlaric was director, Stephen Gregg served as dramaturg, and Chyanne Fischer served as stage manager. The cast was as follows:

MONA	Katelyn Stieg
FINIAN	Joshua Pride
ANGUS	Clayton Sulby
CAITLIN	Brie Greer
MUIRIN	Grae Greer

SKIN was originally performed in the spring of 2014 by Auburn Creative and Performing Arts High School, directed by Joselyn Ludtke and assistant-directed by Derick Edgren. The stage manager was Tatianna Salisbury. The cast was as follows:

OLDER FINIAN	Jacob Herrmann
OLDER MUIRIN	Asia Ward
FINIAN	Mark Salstrand
MUIRIN	Sarah Pfleiderer
MONA	Allison Pitman
ANGUS	Lance Ferguson
CAITLIN	Mackenzie Makela
ROARK	Lucas Wulf
ERIN	Sydney Stewart
SEAN	Nick Cordonnier
FINIAN'S CHILD	Abi Shelton
MUIRIN'S CHILD	Sophie Braman
CORDELIA	Tatianna Salisbury

SKIN was read and developed by Sarah Lawrence College Theatre Department for the First Look Reading Series, under the direction of Edunn Levy, at the Open Space Theater in February, 2015. The play was developed under the watchful eye of faculty member Cassandra Medley. Stage directions were read by Mallory Muratore. The cast was as follows:

FINIAN	Ethan Graham-Horowitz
MUIRIN	Carrigan O'Brian
CAITLIN	Isabella Roland
BRADEN	Maxwell Hegley

ABOUT THE PLAYWRIGHT

Both an essayist and playwright, Derick's plays have been performed in festivals across the country, recognized by theaters such as the West Side Show Room, La Strada Ensemble, and Blank Theater Company. Most recently, his short play *Hydrangea Journal* was produced in the Renaissance Guild's ActOne Series XVIII in San Antonio, and his play *Earth from the Moon* was produced in the Young Actor's Studio's New Works Festival in Hollywood. In addition to being a full-time undergraduate student of English and Theater at Sarah Lawrence College, Derick is also a writer for *College News* and a blog contributor for *Adroit Journal*. He loves white boards and, primarily for that reason, dreams of becoming an educator. "I am forever thankful to and for my mother and father who have encouraged me to pursue the arts from the start, my brothers Lucas and Xavier who always keep it real, my great friend Recha who told me this would happen years ago, and Luke who helped me realized she was right. I love you all."

DEDICATION

For Chimamanda Ngozi Adichie, whose telling of her own story taught me how to love my own, and because maybe if I dedicate a play to her I'll meet her someday.

"I think you travel to search and you come back home to find yourself there."

CHARACTERS

FINIAN – 17, a fisherman. Adventurous.
MUIRIN – A selkie, older than Finian. Doubtful.
CAITLIN – Late 40s, mother of Finian. Manic.
BRADEN – A selkie, same age as Muirin. Happy but distant.

SETTING

Dalkey, Ireland. An old little house set next to a small, rocky shore.

TIME

3 April 1951. 4 April 1958.

AUTHOR'S NOTE

The shore should be placed (by the actors' focus) as if it were in the audience.

(Stage right is a small house, the entrance of which is set profile to the audience so that there is a wall, which has one window, separating indoors and outdoors. Indoors is a sparse but cramped living space. Outdoors is a spacious rocky beach, with a very old rowboat sitting on the shore.)

*(**AT RISE:** Breakfast time, the crack of dawn. **CAITLIN** has tea. She goes through the mail. One envelope seems particularly exciting. **FINIAN** is looking at maps somewhere else in the space.)*

CAITLIN. Finian? Put those maps away and have a cup o' tea and some porridge at the table, there's something I want to show you!

FINIAN. Oh I will. Later.

CAITLIN. Later? That's funny, I don't remember asking you to do it *later*. Probably because later hasn't happened yet and won't happen for…well at least another twelve months judging how many maps you've got out. Besides, you'll be out of the house in a moment, won't you?

FINIAN. Mhm.

CAITLIN. Why so many today?

FINIAN. *("I don't know.")* Iunno.

CAITLIN. You hadn't said a word since you woke up.

FINIAN. Just looking over the plan for today. Oh wait. That hasn't changed for seven years.

CAITLIN. As long as it includes staying off those big motor boats.

FINIAN. That's right. I'll stay on the dock. Like always.

CAITLIN. Well. I suppose you don't really need to be looking at those maps, then. Instead you could have your porridge and tea, right?

FINIAN. Oh, now I can't *look* at the ocean either?

CAITLIN. Finian, please, just sit at the table for one moment, there's something that came in the mail I want to show you.

FINIAN. Maybe I just want it quiet!

CAITLIN. Just want it quiet? You're going to be sitting in your rowboat all day, that's not enough quiet?

FINIAN. Which is just grand fun. Love every bleeding second of sitting in a stale little pond. Brings joy to my heart and meaning to my life. Lots of fish, too!

CAITLIN. Watch it, Finian. Open the letter.

FINIAN. Alright I will, I will.

(He picks up the letter and opens it. He reads.)

CAITLIN. *(Maybe too excited)* We're going to Dublin!!!

FINIAN. Wait I – I don't understand – what is this?

CAITLIN. My cousin Seamus got you a job as a telephone operator! Oh I know the fishing's been miserable for you lately, but now we can finally do something about it.

FINIAN. Just because I don't want to fish doesn't mean I want to be some bleeding telephone operator.

CAITLIN. But, you – oh you're not seeing what I see in this.

FINIAN. No! What about sailing past the cove to explore the ocean! You said we could fix Father's boat and I could –

CAITLIN. I'll pour you some tea.

FINIAN. No. I don't want tea and I don't want to go to Dublin. I want to go out and see the world, Mum. At least see what Father saw out there.

CAITLIN. Which is what?

FINIAN. That's just it, he could never tell me!

(She pours him tea and plans on going to Dublin.)

CAITLIN. A cup o' tea for good luck at sea. That's what your father always said in the mornings, right?

FINIAN. And what are we gonna do with the rowboat? That was *his* rowboat, we can't just get rid of it.

CAITLIN. Well no. But sell it. How much sugar?

FINIAN. Mum!

CAITLIN. *(Spooning sugar into his cup)* Well I can't know how much is right if you don't tell me, lad.

FINIAN. I don't want any bleeding sugar. Mum, we are not getting rid of that boat and we're not going anywhere. We can't just leave this house all of a sudden, it doesn't make sense.

CAITLIN. It hasn't been his in seven years! Drink the tea.

FINIAN. No.

CAITLIN. And get some rest. We leave tomorrow.

FINIAN. What? How?

CAITLIN. Seamus will drive in to pick us up and we'll stay with him until we find a home.

FINIAN. We have a home. You can't do this, Mum. What about Father?

CAITLIN. I talked to Patrick and he's taking the rowboat for parts.

FINIAN. You're disgusting.

CAITLIN. You don't have to like it, Finian. But you have to live it.

FINIAN. We'll see.

(He folds up the maps and walks to the door. There's a letter sitting where they were.)

CAITLIN. What do you think you're doing?

FINIAN. I'm going out in the boat.

CAITLIN. But Finian, you –

FINIAN. Well if it's the last time then it's the last time.

CAITLIN. We have boxes to pack.

FINIAN. I don't care.

CAITLIN. Finian, I –

FINIAN. Forget it. I'll be back.

CAITLIN. Wait! What is this?

FINIAN. For you.

CAITLIN. For me?

FINIAN. It's…the money. From yesterday. But don't open it now.

CAITLIN. Feels light.

FINIAN. Big bills.

CAITLIN. Oh and you better not go past the cove either! I'll be watching to see if you do.

FINIAN. I know you will.

CAITLIN. Wait.

FINIAN. What now?

CAITLIN. You're not leaving without a proper prayer.

FINIAN. I don't need one, I told you, I'm not going far!

CAITLIN. Take my hands.

FINIAN. No Mum.

CAITLIN. There are creatures with evil spirits in those waters, Finian. Those selkies won't hesitate to come after you. Beautiful, they'll draw you in, they will, but once you are in reach, death to your soul.

FINIAN. Mum it's not me you need to convince. It's everyone else.

CAITLIN. Everyone else. What I would give to finally be able to say "everyone else" and mean hundreds of people around me. Soon. Soon. But if it's not you I need to convince, why won't you pray?

FINIAN. *(Closing his eyes, speaking quickly)*
May the blessing of light be upon you,
Light on the outside,
Light on the inside.
With God's sunlight shining on you,
may your heart glow with warmth,
like a turf fire,
that welcomes friends and strangers alike.
May the light of the Lord shine from your eyes,
Like a candle in the window,
welcoming the weary traveler – alright bye.

CAITLIN. Oh wait.

FINIAN. What now!

CAITLIN. It's just, always hard watching you walk out that door. I'm sorry you're upset, but it'll all work out. I promise.

FINIAN. Okay.

CAITLIN. I love you. Be safe.

*(**FINIAN** exits. **CAITLIN** goes to the window and watches him. He puts the maps in the rowboat and pretends to push the rowboat into the water. **CAITLIN**, more at ease, goes to the couch and looks at the envelope **FINIAN** left her. She doesn't open it. Blackout inside the house.)*

*(Aware that his mother is no longer looking, **FINIAN** retrieves a large trunk from a hiding place. He throws the maps inside and pulls out a pocket notebook. He bookmarks a page and puts it in his back pocket. He tosses the chest into the rowboat and gets back in. He does not leave shore just yet. Instead, he takes out the notebook again, and begins writing. It is not necessary that he speak as slowly as he writes. Or perhaps the rowboat prevents us from seeing him actually write this out.)*

FINIAN. 3 April 1951. Dear Father, It's our last day in Dalkey. That's right. Mum finally did it. Got myself a job in Dublin. No, *she* didn't get a job. She got *me* a job…but that's okay, because I decided I'm leaving home. I'm running away! I'm gonna take the rowboat beyond our cove just like you promised we could one day… I wish you were here to see me do it. I brought all your maps and gear and I caught myself some cod so I wouldn't starve, of course. I feel bad about leaving Mum, but she wouldn't have wanted to come. She doesn't understand like you did. I hate fishing, but I don't want to go to the city. So I left her a letter explaining everything. I think she can take my job in the city, and she'll be happier there. I'll let you know where I end up. But for now, I'm just going to go away – to the ocean! Here I go! Love, Finian.

(He puts the notebook away. He gets up and tries to push the boat into the water but, as he does, something slams into the bow.)

Jaysus! What the hell was that? Better not have broke the...

(A woman lies in the water, a great pelt-looking cloak on top of her.)

Oh bleeding – uh, lass? Lass!

(Her head moves. She is badly injured by the impact of the rowboat.)

Oh no are you alright, let me...Wait – wait a – you're not – you! You're a selkie! A bleeding selkie! Stay back!

MUIRIN. Please.

*(**FINIAN** reaches into the trunk in the rowboat and removes a fishing rod. It's a weapon now. He swings it at her. She gasps.)*

(Choking for air) No!

FINIAN. Get back! Get back now!

(She growls at him, big-eyed, but still hurt.)

MUIRIN. *(Difficult to understand)* Skin.

FINIAN. I said get back.

MUIRIN. Skin!

FINIAN. I'll really hurt you, I will!

*(She tries to lift her sealskin for him to see. He whips her with the hook of his fishing rod, and she cries out. **FINIAN** is still cautious.)*

What do you want from us? What else do you want to take from us? Take our food? Our money? Take everything, then!

(He reaches into his trunk and throws bait at her.)

Just take it all, that's what you do, right? You thieve and you lie and you kill like bleeding sirens on the rocks – humans are your game. I know!

MUIRIN. C-c-c...cold.

FINIAN. You think I'm supposed to pity you? Tell me. Where are the rest? Are they close?

MUIRIN. Broken...you...broke.

FINIAN. I didn't break the bleeding boat, you did! Because you're evil!

MUIRIN. *(Shaking her head)* Skin...

FINIAN. What, your...your sealskin? Is that what that is?

(She nods, trying to stand.)

Oughta teach you a lesson, then. Make an example of you!

(He faces the open water.)

D'you all see that? You bleeding selkies! *(To her.)* Now you know what it's like to be taken from home and from family. Seeing as how you look now, selkies don't last on land for very long.

MUIRIN. I...don't know.

FINIAN. Let's find out, then.

MUIRIN. Please...

FINIAN. Good riddance.

*(She collapses again, wheezing, coughing, making inhuman noises. It is a slow, painful death. And **FINIAN** watches as she dies. He does not leave, but he does not help. He can only think to stand and watch.)*

MUIRIN. *(Barely audible)* You...father...

FINIAN. What?

MUIRIN. Father! Your father! ...drowned.

FINIAN. What are you blatherin' about now?

(She closes her eyes.)

What do you know about my father? Hey! Wake up! What do I do?

*(**FINIAN** takes her skin. There's a big tear in it.)*

This. You want me to fix this?

(He gets some fish hooks out of the trunk and starts to "stitch" the sealskin closed. She reacts every time as if she were being pricked with a needle.)

Just one more...is that better? Hello? What about my father?

MUIRIN. What did you do? Where did you...

FINIAN. Tell me what you know about my father.

MUIRIN. He is a fisherman.

FINIAN. No. He was a fisherman. He was killed seven years ago.

MUIRIN. He...is alive.

FINIAN. What? *(Beat.)* No.

MUIRIN. Yes.

FINIAN. How would you know that?

MUIRIN. Please. *(Re: fish hooks)* This will not last long. Help me fix it.

FINIAN. He can't be alive, he – he would have come looking for us. He would have come home.

MUIRIN. No. He's trapped in a cave, right around that cliff.

FINIAN. All this time? But...that can't be. Can it? No.

MUIRIN. We bring him fresh water, and he fishes for his food. I saw you leaving and I thought I would tell you. But now my skin has been ruined and I have to –

FINIAN. He's been there *all* this time and no one has ever found him?

MUIRIN. I'm sorry.

FINIAN. And you never said anything?

MUIRIN. I was prohibited – it's not allowed for me to be on land. I shouldn't right now, but –

FINIAN. I have to tell Mum.

MUIRIN. NO! Please don't! No one can know I'm on land.

FINIAN. ...Why? Is it your fault?

MUIRIN. No.

FINIAN. Because she'd kill you if that were true! She'd wring you out to dry and you'd never feel the wetness

of your precious sea ever again. I would do it, too.
Why shouldn't I? Why shouldn't I kill you? I have to
do something...

MUIRIN. If you kill me, how will you find him?

(Her breathing is heavy. FINIAN *takes off his jacket and wraps it around her.)*

FINIAN. He's really alive. You know it's him.

MUIRIN. I used to see you out here with him.

FINIAN. Then I'll help you. For now.

MUIRIN. I need warmth.

FINIAN. I'll bring you warmth. Clothing.

MUIRIN. Fire.

FINIAN. What?

MUIRIN. Fire.

FINIAN. I can't bring you fire.

MUIRIN. You need your father. I need fire.

FINIAN. Alright then I'll bring you fire! Anything else?
How 'bout a cup o' tea while I'm at it? Jaysus, let's
see...

(He tosses a shirt, a pair of pants, and a sweater at her.)

Put those clothes on, would you?

(She doesn't move.)

Oh, and uh...are you hungry?

(He tosses her an orange.)

For trying to kill you. Sorry about that...

(She doesn't touch it.)

I'm telling you, lass, you'll freeze your arse off if you
don't put those on. Now let's see, I don't think I have
any wood here...I don't know what to tell you, if you
don't move in five seconds I'm gonna have to –

MUIRIN. I'm cold.

FINIAN. Did you not hear me say those clothes are for you
the first two times?

(She looks at the clothes on the ground like they are an unappetizing meal.)

That's right. For you.

MUIRIN. I need warmth.

FINIAN. That's what I'm trying to provide you with, lass, but you won't let me! You know I have somewhere to be now. If you say my father's out there then I have to go find him and rescue him. And I would hate to go to all this trouble just for you to freeze to death. *(Picking up clothing.)* So take these and put them on.

MUIRIN. I…

FINIAN. Okay, then. Why don't you just…sit still.

(He slowly lifts his jacket off of her and helps her put on the clothing – she may wince occasionally should they make direct contact.)

Sensitive skin.

(She tries to know what she is doing.)

Arms through the sleeves…that's it. You never seen someone put on clothes before?

(He puts on the shirt and two large sweaters.)

Or never dressed yourself before?

(She shakes her head.)

Well next comes the pants so you'll need to sit up.

MUIRIN. Okay.

(The cold has really gotten to her.)

FINIAN. Hold onto me. Put your legs through here. And here.

(She puts her hands on his shoulders and slips into the pants. If she falls, he catches her.)

MUIRIN. Thank you.

(They stare at each other.)

FINIAN. Well there are you, lass.

MUIRIN. My name is Muirin.

FINIAN. I'm Finian. I know this is all new to you but humans like to learn names *before* seeing each other naked. Most of the time. *(Beat.)* That was a joke. Selkies know about jokes underwater? You're supposed to laugh at them.

MUIRIN. *(Not finding it funny)* Oh.

(FINIAN demonstrates laughter.)

FINIAN. Ring any bells? No? Alright. You know, you're different than I thought you would be. Selkies. Sel-kies. Seems like there's a lot I don't know. *(Beat.)* Why aren't you saying anything?

MUIRIN. You think more is better, but that is not always true.

FINIAN. Well, more than just, enough to get by. If you're just getting by that's no life at all, that's survival, lass. Trust me, I would know. Been fishing out here alone every day for seven years. I wake up, I see my mum, I fish, go to bed, the end. It's lonely. There aren't many roads so there aren't many people. Don't see a lot of people. Just my mum – and I was trying to get away from her before you came around. To run away. To be like my father, but, I guess now I can be *with* him. You see this notebook? It's filled with letters to him. I started doing this after I thought he was…gone, and I've got dozens of them in this trunk. But now he can read them, can't he?

MUIRIN. I think so.

FINIAN. I just – I remember when I was nine and we were out here fishing – nothing big, no nets, just rods, and, I looked out past that cliff there, and I asked my father what was out there, out in the ocean. And he told me he didn't know. I thought he knew everything. But he said we could find out together, *that* was grand. And well, the time came but, he's not here. Mum would never let me out of the cove since. But what about him? Is everything alright?

MUIRIN. Oh yes.

FINIAN. Does he talk about me? You said sometimes you watch me, do you do it because he asks about me?

MUIRIN. Well…

FINIAN. Tell me everything.

MUIRIN. But you have to help me first. To fix my skin.

FINIAN. Fix your – what makes you think I can do that?

MUIRIN. You don't have a choice. I need things only you can get. You have to understand that –

FINIAN. Well now you're talking just fine, aren't you.

MUIRIN. You don't know anything about us. You're all ignorant.

FINIAN. You can't expect us to know if you keep your gob shut all the time.

MUIRIN. You have to fix the skin tonight or I can never go back.

FINIAN. Why didn't you tell me that first?

MUIRIN. Because you would have tried to destroy it. *(Beat.)* I have to go back as soon as possible. I'm getting married tomorrow.

FINIAN. You seem pretty chuffed about it, lass.

MUIRIN. His name is Braden.

FINIAN. Well how did you end up here when you have a fella at home?

MUIRIN. I had always wanted to see what it was like on land.

FINIAN. Let me be the first to tell you, Muirin. There's not much to it.

MUIRIN. I watch you fish. And you sit in your boat for hours in the middle of the water. But you don't ever pay attention to the net. You're staring out at sea, like you can see something out there. Something beautiful, even if you don't know what it is yet. If you're going to go out there, you'll need to repair that boat. I know the story of your father because it is often told to me, and I know the ocean. Fix my skin and I can guide you to him.

FINIAN. But how?

(MUIRIN gently picks up her skin in her arms and lays it down flat, smoothing it out with her hands as her fingers run along the surface.)

MUIRIN. *(Looking to the sea)* Whatever your mother has told you is not true.

FINIAN. Then what's true?

MUIRIN. When a selkie loses her skin, it is because a fisherman has taken it from her. Without it whole, she is not whole, and she cannot return to the sea. And if she does not mend it before the next moonrise, then she never will.

FINIAN. So you're saying we have to do this by –

MUIRIN. Midnight. Yes.

FINIAN. Well it better not be some grand trek!

MUIRIN. *Seid fola, chailfidh deora, chaillfidh solas.*

FINIAN. Huh?

MUIRIN. Shed blood, shed tears, shed light.

FINIAN. What's that?

MUIRIN. That is how we heal any wound.

FINIAN. I don't get it.

(MUIRIN stands and, her cut still fresh, lets the blood drip into the water.)

MUIRIN. From your hook.

FINIAN. Sorry.

MUIRIN. When there is blood, there is pain. Any wound comes with pain.

FINIAN. What do you mean?

MUIRIN. When someone hurts you, three things happen. You bleed. You cry. And you grow.

FINIAN. You think it's that simple.

MUIRIN. I know it is.

FINIAN. And what does that have to do with your skin?

MUIRIN. I've given to the water one of three things I need to return whole. It is an offering to the open sea. When it is complete, my love and my family will come for me. A drop of my blood, seven tears of a human woman, and...

FINIAN. Light! How the hell are we supposed to *give* light to the bleeding ocean?

MUIRIN. Don't worry about that now. Your mother. Where is she?

FINIAN. Inside. Why?

MUIRIN. You must make her weep and catch her tears in a cup. Then you must bring it here.

FINIAN. You want to make my mother cry.

MUIRIN. It is the only way.

FINIAN. How the hell d'you suppose I go about that, then?

MUIRIN. It is up to you, Finian, so that you may find your father. And so that I may return to the sea and marry.

FINIAN. Well my mum's no stone but far from a peach either.

MUIRIN. You must! She is the only one near, is she not? The only one you speak to?

FINIAN. Yeah...just, tears? That's all it is?

MUIRIN. They must be of sadness. When we are wounded, we weep.

FINIAN. Yeah yeah and you'll tell me how to get to my father safely?

MUIRIN. Yes.

FINIAN. How do you know for sure, then?

MUIRIN. I trusted you. Now you must do the same.

FINIAN. Trust a selkie, I should? You think just because I helped you out of the water and gave you some sweaters all is grand now? That I'm suddenly on your side? Because that's not what I think. I think you're a selfish creature who just wants her skin so she can go get bleeding married and kill more sailors and fisherman when they get the chance.

MUIRIN. We are not violent.

FINIAN. But you are killers! Admit it!

MUIRIN. I will not! I told you, Finian, I will do what I can for you, but you must do the same for me. I have already bled for you.

FINIAN. You didn't bleed for me, you bled *because* of me.

MUIRIN. Is that supposed to sound better?

FINIAN. I liked it better when you talked less.

MUIRIN. You still don't believe me.

FINIAN. I don't have a real reason to.

MUIRIN. He says this about you to my father. That you are adventurous, a curious mind. And you dream of traveling the world by boat someday. That you will, he knows you will because you see it before it happens. And that he wishes to travel with you, far beyond this cove, into other worlds that you would never imagine were real.

FINIAN. He…he said that?

MUIRIN. Yes, Finian.

FINIAN. *(Truly believing her now)* He misses me, then. He really misses me. I wonder what that's like, being trapped in a wee cavern. Bet he hates it, doesn't he?

MUIRIN. Yes. He wishes to see you.

FINIAN. You said it's against the rules for you to be out of water. And you're getting married tomorrow. So…why are you here now?

MUIRIN. Because I had always wanted to leave home, too. Ever since I was a wee lass and came above water onto the rocks and could see thin shadows walking on land. Even after my mother and father told me they were dangerous, I – I couldn't stay away because, as afraid as I was of what they could have been, I was more afraid of never finding out.

FINIAN. Oh. Wow…well, that's. That's grand.

MUIRIN. D'you see those low rocks at the bottom of that cliff, Finian?

FINIAN. Yes.

MUIRIN. Do you know about those rocks?

FINIAN. I know they're where my father crashed.

MUIRIN. Above the waves are calm, but underneath there are strong currents going in many directions. I think that life can be like that. It is never truly static. And, those rocks are what you must learn to navigate to get out of this cove alive. And I can teach you. There is a right way, and there is a wrong way.

FINIAN. I knew that much. How else would my father have made it past?

MUIRIN. Right.

FINIAN. But I want to hear more details.

MUIRIN. I've said enough. Now it's your turn. The tears.

FINIAN. But I told you, I ran away from home. I can never see her again!

MUIRIN. Bring them here. Tonight.

*(Short blackout. Then, we see **FINIAN** entering his home, which now has various boxes scattered about. His mother is going through them.)*

FINIAN. Mum?

*(**CAITLIN** immediately bursts into loud, messy tears.)*

Hi.

CAITLIN. Oh there you are! Did you go down to the dock? To say goodbye?

FINIAN. Yeah I did.

CAITLIN. Good.

*(She gets really close to him as she cleans. **FINIAN** picks up her tea cup and puts it behind his back.)*

FINIAN. Why are you crying, Mum?

CAITLIN. Crying, oh, you think I'm crying? Oh no no, I'm just going through these boxes, so excited for the change in our lives. A change for us both, together.

FINIAN. You should sit down. You don't look well.

CAITLIN. Oh but I'm grand, Finian, really.

(She still moves around the space more than necessary. Every time she opens a box she gets more upset. Each time he tries to put the cup under her eyes, whether she notices it or not, **CAITLIN** *swats the cup away.)*

FINIAN. Here. Do you need help? Why don't you sit with your tea?

CAITLIN. Oh no Finian the cup's empty now, though.

FINIAN. We'll fill it again later.

CAITLIN. I know what you're doing, Finian.

FINIAN. *(Slowing down)* You do?

CAITLIN. Yes! But I'm not upset!

FINIAN. You're not?

CAITLIN. Why would I be? …You know you gave me the money from yesterday. That's a very funny letter you wrote. My son wants to run away to become a sailor… but without a sailboat. I thought I told you we were leaving, though. Together.

FINIAN. You read the letter.

CAITLIN. And I always thought you might want to go and look for him, but I didn't think you'd ever try it. Well, I'm glad you're back. Because we have some more packing to do. It's gonna take all day…

FINIAN. Oh Mum I –

CAITLIN. *(Still bawling)* You have to learn to move on, Finian. That letter – I understand, I do, that you want to go out and understand but sometimes there's nothing more to understand, really. It just happened. And now this is happening. We are leaving. Together. Your father was a great man, a hero, and a brilliant fisherman. But seven years is a long time. And he's gone now, and without him there's nothing for us here. You have to realize that, no matter how hard it might be.

FINIAN. Mum please, just – just sit for a moment, I know it's hard.

CAITLIN. I know you don't like the idea of the city but I thought it could be good to move on. Your father would want that for us, right? Because I would give the little we have here to be, the three of us again. So when I sit in this house and I look out that window I don't see one body. I see two, like I should. Not one. I wish for him back, I do!

FINIAN. *(About to tell her)* Maybe – um...

CAITLIN. Maybe what?

FINIAN. Maybe...maybe we *can* move on. But it will take time.

(They sit. He gives her the tea cup. She cradles it in her hands. She cries softly, looking down.)

CAITLIN. *(Calmer)* I watch you turn into him year after year. Taking his maps into your room and locking yourself in there for hours with those maps and the notebooks and all of it. But the sea is a dangerous, evil place Finian. I won't say their name aloud, but they are cruel and wild animals, and you know what they did to your father, and you should never forget that. No matter what anyone else says about him drowning, we, we know what happened that day – and, if you were to go out there, too, and – you could, could...

*(**FINIAN** takes the cup from her and stands. He walks away.)*

He's still there.

FINIAN. What?

CAITLIN. Every box is another piece of him. It's like he's still here, but he can't be himself again. He's trying to return to it but he can't. Do you ever feel that, love?

FINIAN. Yes.

*(**CAITLIN** takes a compass out of one of the boxes.)*

CAITLIN. It was his. Hold onto it...

FINIAN. Okay.

*(**FINIAN** steps away.)*

CAITLIN. Where are you going?

FINIAN. Make sure I tied up the boat, is all.

CAITLIN. And that's it.

FINIAN. Yes.

CAITLIN. Oh. We'll finish up these boxes when you come back, then?

FINIAN. Uh huh.

CAITLIN. You will come back this time, won't you?

FINIAN. *(Hesitant)* …Yes.

CAITLIN. *(Trying to smile)* Alright. Goodbye for now.

(She goes back to the boxes in a daze.)

FINIAN. Goodbye, Mum.

(FINIAN exits to the outdoors.)

(MUIRIN is going through the trunk.)

Here. Take them.

MUIRIN. Already? You mean it wasn't – ?

FINIAN. What the hell are you doing?

MUIRIN. Was this all his?

FINIAN. I said get away, don't touch any of that!

(She has one of his notebooks, an older one.)

Hand that over right now. How long have you had that? Hand it over right now!

MUIRIN. I'm sorry, I just wanted to see what you –

FINIAN. It's not yours to see, alright? It's –

MUIRIN. Letters to your father. I think they're beautiful, Finian.

FINIAN. Yeah, well…

MUIRIN. Could you read one to me? I think I understand, but it's hard to learn to read when you're, well, underwater.

FINIAN. No kidding.

(He flips through it.)

Well, I guess I could… You picked out an older one. Oh. Here. *(Reading)* 13 September 1947. I didn't want to go to school today – *(to MUIRIN)* oh this is back a ways – *(Reading)* but I feel grand that I did. There was a fierce fog and it was raining, but Mary shared her umbrella with me…

(He stops.)

MUIRIN. Oh why did you stop? That sounded so sweet!

FINIAN. What's the point really? Just some girl I once knew. Only people I ever see now are down at the harbor, and all they want is my fish.

MUIRIN. Did you love her?

FINIAN. Well, I – no, it was… I was just a boy, then… And what about your fella? What ever happened to that, you haven't said much about him.

MUIRIN. *(Her tone changes.)* It's not just a marriage. It's different than what you think.

FINIAN. Then what is it?

MUIRIN. Maybe I was trying to run away, too.

FINIAN. Huh?

MUIRIN. Because we don't marry for love like that, Finian. It is for safety and for more children and that is all.

FINIAN. So you don't love him?

MUIRIN. Do you know what love is? According to that notebook you're not so sure!

FINIAN. Well do you?

MUIRIN. I care for him.

FINIAN. That's not what I asked.

(MUIRIN coughs.)

MUIRIN. Let me see them, the tears. Please.

(He gives them to her. She closes her eyes and pours them into the water.)

FINIAN. Well? Now what? Will it work?

MUIRIN. Shed blood, shed tears, shed light –

FINIAN. Shed light, I know – isn't that so you can have three things to say? You don't really expect me to find you some pint of light, do you?

MUIRIN. That's not what it means.

FINIAN. Then what the bleeding hell does it mean?

MUIRIN. Wait. Do you see that?

FINIAN. I'm getting real tired of wading through this pig shite –

MUIRIN. Oh I see them! On the rocks. There they are, right there!

FINIAN. See what?

MUIRIN. Help me up. It's getting harder to stay upright.

FINIAN. Who is it?

MUIRIN. Braden and the others. Home.

(He helps her up and she waves at them.)

Hello! Hello! Do you think they see us? Hello!

FINIAN. I don't know.

MUIRIN. Hey!

FINIAN. Muirin.

MUIRIN. HEY!

FINIAN. Shhh, my mum's right over there, she'll hear us and come out here.

MUIRIN. But they don't see me.

FINIAN. They'll find you later.

MUIRIN. Later?

FINIAN. Well they probably don't recognize you like this.

MUIRIN. Well then I have to shout!

FINIAN. No!

(He covers her mouth until she loosens herself out of his grip and falls to the ground, her breathing heavy. Seals bark in the distance.)

Do you really even want to go back?

MUIRIN. What?

FINIAN. You didn't think they wouldn't recognize you? Why do you want to go back?

MUIRIN. Well, I – I have to. For Braden. For my parents, my –

FINIAN. What about you?

MUIRIN. Me? *(Realizing something.)* Oh no.

FINIAN. I understand your concern and all, but I think maybe – well – what if you came with me on the boat, to find my father…and then you stayed here?

MUIRIN. Here?

FINIAN. Well not here. With us. In the city.

MUIRIN. Finian, it doesn't work like that. I have to be in the water, to live. If I lose my skin tonight, I'll never have the choice to go back.

FINIAN. We could get you something! A bathtub, maybe, just for you. And maybe if you stay, maybe you won't miss it. Maybe you would become healthy. And the waves, they would still be there for you, just not for you to be *in*. And we could tell my father about you and maybe my mother, too – it would be hard for her to swallow at first but if we just explained all this to her, I wouldn't mind you… I don't mind you. In fact, I think… I think you're –

MUIRIN. No, Finian, you have to stop thinking like that. I still have to go and we need to finish this. The light, we need to find the light.

FINIAN. But Muirin, I really think you should think about it! My father's not like me, he doesn't get angry a lot, I know I do, and I don't know why but I think maybe –

MUIRIN. I can't, Finian, I just can't. Now this light, it's something new, something learned. You must grow, remember?

FINIAN. I don't think I understand –

MUIRIN. And sometimes to grow you don't exactly get what you want.

FINIAN. What are you saying, Muirin? A life lesson? How is that gonna fix your skin?

MUIRIN. *(Nervous)* The light will shine, through and, and fix everything. I promise. And I have to learn mine, too…

FINIAN. Learn what?

MUIRIN. *(In a lot of pain)* It's getting late. I have to tell you something, Finian.

FINIAN. I'm right here.

MUIRIN. I'm sorry.

FINIAN. About what?

MUIRIN. Our deal will still stand, though.

FINIAN. Just tell me.

MUIRIN. You promise to see the light in this?

FINIAN. YES! Now what the hell –

MUIRIN. Your father is dead.

FINIAN. He…what?

MUIRIN. Let me explain.

FINIAN. Did you kill him?

MUIRIN. Finian, wait, let me –

FINIAN. So you made it all up, then, huh? You're a monster. And you were there, weren't you?

MUIRIN. He was trying to take my parents, Finian! He was coming after us, to take my mother and kill my father.

FINIAN. You're lying again!!!

MUIRIN. This is the truth! And, he was trying because he knew what we were, Finian. He always did, that's why he went so far out to sea and fished away from the harbor. He saw it in our eyes. And so we lured his ship into the rocks because otherwise he would have killed us. We had no choice. So, yes, I lied to you about your father, but like I said it's the light that we can –

FINIAN. SHUT UP! Before I knock the living daylights out of you!

MUIRIN. And you must learn to be with your mother – wait no please!

(He is just about to punch her.)

I'm sorry, Finian.

(He picks up her skin and tears it. She screams in agony. He tears it again, and her body contorts itself. She bleeds.)

FINIAN. What am I supposed to do now! I wrote all those letters, and he was going to read them. You said he'd read them!

(He tears it again.)

MUIRIN. *(Gasping)* Please stop!

FINIAN. Why did you come here?! Why! To kill me next? Or just to have a laugh, maybe? Laugh at the fisherman with his crazy mum struggling to stay afloat after his father died! I can't believe I actually believed you to begin with, you sick creature! All this time you're just looking out for yourself – it doesn't make any bleeding sense for you to be here! Just, rub it in, you've got family and your husband and the sea you love so much, so why'd you leave it! Tell me! Why!

MUIRIN. *(Still out of breath)* I came for you!

*(**FINIAN** stops tearing the skin.)*

I longed to meet you, Finian. I was tired and I was curious. Sometimes the waves fall silent and the water is still, and there is nothing for us to push against anymore. I needed that again. Braden is a wave, but you, are like a hurricane. I'm told the story of your father year after year, to avoid humans, to run from humans, but I've always thought about you, about being with you.

FINIAN. But you don't know me!

MUIRIN. But I do. I've watched you. I have known you all these years. I have known your eyes and I have known your smile, gazing out at sea. I've known your loss, how you wish to go far away from home, to sail away and start life somewhere where the pain does not risk drowning you… And I have known that I would like that, too. To sail away.

FINIAN. But I…

MUIRIN. I wanted to understand you.

FINIAN. And now you do.

MUIRIN. I'm sorry, Finian. I did not mean to hurt you. Just, please, at least help me return to what I know before it's too late.

(**FINIAN** *is still unsure.*)

If you will not, then I must sing.

FINIAN. I don't understand.

MUIRIN. A song is often meant for endings, is it not?

(**MUIRIN** *inches closer to the water, and begins oohing "An Irish Blessing." He stands still as she does, eventually caving in to help her. The sound of seals barking. Maybe they hear* **MUIRIN**'s *song.*)

FINIAN. What do I have to do?

(**CAITLIN** *bursts through the front door and charges at them.*)

CAITLIN. I knew it!

FINIAN. Wait –

CAITLIN. You fowl, fowl creature, what have you done to my boy to make him want to leave his mother!

FINIAN. Mum, no!

(**FINIAN** *catches* **CAITLIN**. *She tries to fight him away.*)

CAITLIN. You wish to lure him away as well, you do! Well I'll see to it, we'll hang you up right at the top of that cliff, draw you up and let them all know that it won't happen. Not again! God help us, let every breath you take grow smaller than the one before!

FINIAN. It wasn't her, Mum.

CAITLIN. You drove him to madness? Having him believe your lies, you did! No! He won't be like his father anymore! Finian, we have to cleanse your spirit and by the grace of God you'll escape the demon inside that ugly beast, I swear to it! Get the rosary now!

FINIAN. You can't hurt her, she didn't do it – she's dying, we have to help her.

CAITLIN. You will not speak those words anymore, I'VE HAD IT! Now let me go!

FINIAN. I won't.

CAITLIN. Because you don't love me? Because you want to run away!

(He pushes his mother back.)

FINIAN. Because I care for her! There's no one else around I can talk to or be honest with or anything! So I care for her.

CAITLIN. More than me?

FINIAN. I care for you, Mum. More than Father ever did.

CAITLIN. You promise?

FINIAN. I promise.

*(And suddenly, **MUIRIN**'s sealskin begins to glow, and mend itself. The tears in the skin reverse, and now it rests on **MUIRIN**'s limp body. She rises, it hanging from her shoulders. She looks at **FINIAN**, still glowing. **FINIAN** begins to glow, too. Even **CAITLIN** glows. They are light, shining against the foggy shore, and this may be a literal glow.)*

MUIRIN. The light. I told you it would come.

*(**FINIAN** and **MUIRIN** fall in love. Everything glows.)*

Seven years. I can return in seven years…will you be here, then?

FINIAN. We'll be in the city… But…yes. I can. I'll be here.

MUIRIN. Right here?

FINIAN. Yes.

MUIRIN. And we can sail away together.

FINIAN. I'd like that.

MUIRIN. Good. *(Beat.)* Goodbye, Finian.

FINIAN. Goodbye, Muirin.

(Seals bark again, closer.)

(MUIRIN puts on her skin and transforms into what looks like an ordinary seal. She is light. And then the light disappears as she does, and all is back to the way it was. Maybe.)

(CAITLIN hugs FINIAN, and he hugs her back. He gives her a nod and, after a moment, they walk inside.)

(Waves.)

(blackout)

(Seven years pass.)

*(**MUIRIN** enters, in her human form.)*

MUIRIN. Hello? Finian? Finian! I've returned! Where are you? Finian…

(She runs to the house, smiling until she opens the door, and finds it empty. Save for a letter, sitting on the ground. She runs back outside.)

Oh very funny! I can't bring a letter home with me. You know I can't do that, it's just going to melt away in the water and… FINIAN! *(No answer.)* Do you think I'm some – desperate, caffler? Stop hiding! I know you're here. *(But he's not.)* Is this all a JOKE to you? I remember your joke! The one about me without, clothes, and…oh what… *(She can't remember the joke.)* Well this one isn't funny either, I remember that much! Oh…alright. This better be good. *(Opening the letter)* Really.

*(She drops the envelope. When she does, **FINIAN** stands behind her – and speaks the letter. He might look at her, but she does not look at him. He's not really there.)*

(She opens it and finds a couple of small pieces of paper ripped from a notebook.)

FINIAN. 2 April 1958. Dear Muirin, Well I don't know what I expected. Seven years is a long time. A long time to wait for someone, and a long time for anything, really. And so I did wait. For seven years. And once, well more like a couple times, but one time I remember really well, there was this lass at the pub and I think she worked in the same building I did. I really wanted to talk to her, to buy her a drink. But I couldn't. I just couldn't. I don't know, it was just a feeling, a little feeling like this stone in my gut, that you put there, and every time I try to talk to another lass it gets bigger and rises in my throat but it never comes out. And so I'm doing this, but after seven years, I don't know why anymore. I can't believe I let you do this

– I guess that's what happens you the only lass you're talking to is your mum…you don't know what you're doing, or why… I stopped writing to my father, too. And I think this is the last letter I ever want to write. Because what good is it doing me, you know? But I just wanted you to know that I was here, seven years later…As much as I write in these little notebooks I can never put down the right words. Maybe in seven more years…something'll be different. Finian.

(He fades away. **MUIRIN** *drops the papers.)*

MUIRIN. Oh no… He was here…and I just missed him! He was here. Right here…oh my…what am I doing here? Have I gone crazy? I…

(The wind blows and she shivers. **BRADEN** *enters.)*

BRADEN. Muirin. What are you doing?

MUIRIN. Nothing.

BRADEN. Come. You'll freeze.

MUIRIN. Will you hold me, then?

BRADEN. Finian is asking for you again. He wants to come on land but I told him not until he's older. What do you think's a good age for him? Muirin?

MUIRIN. Just hold me.

(He holds her.)

Braden?

BRADEN. Yes.

MUIRIN. Will you love me in seven years?

BRADEN. Why would you ask that?

MUIRIN. Seven years is a long time. A long time to love someone, and a long time for anything, really.

BRADEN. Yes. It is.

(He doesn't know what else to say.)

MUIRIN. Come. We'll freeze.

The End

www.ingramcontent.com/pod-product-compliance
Lightning Source LLC
Chambersburg PA
CBHW051453290426
44109CB00016B/1739